W9-BOB-363

PETA's VEGAN COLLEGE COOKBOOK

275 EASY, CHEAP, AND DELICIOUS RECIPES TO KEEP YOU VEGAN AT SCHOOL

PEOPLE FOR THE ETHICAL TREATMENT OF ANIMALS

WITH MARTA HOLMBERG AND STARZA KOLMAN

sourcebooks

Copyright © 2016 by People for the Ethical Treatment of Animals
Cover and internal design © 2016 by Sourcebooks, Inc.
Cover design by Sourcebooks, Inc.
Cover images © benhammad/Getty Images, mayakova/Getty Images,
Kevin Summers/Getty Images, Danya Weiner/Getty Images,
Tastyart Ltd Rob White/Getty Images, enviromantic/Getty Images
Internal images © kondratya/Getty Images, Oksancia/Getty Images,
Nataleana/Getty Images
Recipe photos by PETA

Sourcebooks and the colophon are registered trademarks of Sourcebooks, Inc.

All rights reserved. No part of this book may be reproduced in any form or by
any electronic or mechanical means including information storage and retrieval
systems—except in the case of brief quotations embodied in critical articles or
reviews—without permission in writing from its publisher, Sourcebooks, Inc.

This publication is designed to provide accurate and authoritative information in
regard to the subject matter covered. It is sold with the understanding that the
publisher is not engaged in rendering legal, accounting, or other professional
service. If legal advice or other expert assistance is required, the services of a
competent professional person should be sought.—*From a Declaration of Principles
Jointly Adopted by a Committee of the American Bar Association and a Committee
of Publishers and Associations*

This book is not intended as a substitute for medical advice from a qualified
physician. The intent of this book is to provide accurate general information in
regard to the subject matter covered. If medical advice or other expert help is
needed, the services of an appropriate medical professional should be sought.

All brand names and product names used in this book are trademarks, registered
trademarks, or trade names of their respective holders. Sourcebooks, Inc., is not
associated with any product or vendor in this book.

Published by Sourcebooks, Inc.
P.O. Box 4410, Naperville, Illinois 60567-4410
(630) 961-3900
Fax: (630) 961-2168
www.sourcebooks.com

This edition issued based on the paperback edition published in 2009 in the United
States by Sourcebooks, Inc.

Library of Congress Cataloging-in-Publication data for the first edition is on file with
the publisher.

Printed and bound in the United States of America.
VP 10 9 8 7 6 5 4 3 2 1

Dedicated to peta2, the youth division of People
for the Ethical Treatment of Animals (PETA), which
has been spicing things up since 2002.

CONTENTS

VI

FOREWORD

From Ingrid E. Newkirk,
President of PETA

WHEN I WAS YOUNG, I WENT TO SCHOOL IN A TOTALLY scary boarding convent run by mean nuns who dressed like Darth Vader and gave us food that was like something from a prison. The boarding school was stuck in the everlasting snows of the Himalayan Mountains, so it was really pretty if you looked outside the window but really ugly when you looked down at your plate. Maybe the cooks hated us or something, but we were served weird dishes like hairy okra in white sauce (which I often stuck in my pocket and snuck out of the dining hall, because the nuns made us eat everything or we'd get it again for as many meals as it took for us to finish it). I remember (vividly) a gruel optimistically called "pepper water," which consisted of water, yes, and some chili paste, yes, and tamarind roots. If you have ever had Vegemite and hated it, avoid tamarind root. One day, some of us raided the teachers' kitchen and made off with a can of peaches that we opened with a boat hook. We were so excited. It's a wonder any of us survived.

Striking out on my own didn't improve my food situation much. Being raised in a food environment like that convent was like getting cooking lessons from electric eels. In fact, there was a Dutch girl in my dorm who used to lie awake at night and talk about how much she missed jellied eels. That's probably what first made me think that being a vegetarian sounded pretty good. Anyway, what did I know about cooking? A big, fat nothing.

And back then, microwaves were something engineers discussed in science magazines.

So I learned to boil water and throw things in it and cry a lot. If friends came over, I would cook multiple dishes and take them out of the oven, some burned, some done, and some raw. That wasn't much fun, but I got invited over to their places a lot, which would have been a cunning plan if it had been a plan.

Later came the hippie food co-ops, where you could actually get things like soy milk but with a slight snag: you had to mix it yourself. Yes, they would sell you soy milk *powder*, and your job was to take it home, find a whisk, and whip it up into something drinkable. I bow down to you, Silk.

So now I live in food heaven. Vegan world. Land of convenience. Home of stuff-yourself-silly-and-still-be-healthy, ethical, happy, and environmentally sane. Thanks to Starza and Marta, who compiled and wrote this book, and the PETA food elves, your dorm life can now be perfect. If something gets you down, just open this book and be comforted within minutes—maybe seconds. And speaking of seconds, yes, please, we'd like some more.

ACKNOWLEDGMENTS

A SPECIAL THANKS TO: REBECCA FISCHER, LARA Sanders, and Patricia Trostle for their invaluable assistance throughout the entire cookbook writing process. To Dan Shannon, Joel Bartlett, Ryan Huling, Chris Garcia, and P. J. Smith for their guidance and input. To Becky Fenson, Amy Elizabeth, Heidi Parker, and Lindsay Pollard-Post for their amazing ability to capture the college voice. And Amy deserves a second shout-out: thank-you for all of your help and for being awesome! To Blake Simmons and Laura Brown for their organizational and research abilities. And to the following people for lending us their recipes, opinions, and taste buds in order to make this book come to life:

Claire Marlatt, Christine Doré, Rachelle Owen, Jennifer Cierlitsky, Alka Chandna, David Perle, Kelly Respess, Paul Kercheval, Chris Holbein, Jenny Lou and Josh Browning, Sean Conner, Caleb Wheeldon, Michael Croland, Teresa Cooper, Christine Tynes, Sarah Pearson, Megan Hartman, Karen Porreca, Patti Tillotson, Meg Caskey, Kelli Provencio, Colleen Higgins, Roxanne Conwell, Jannette Patterson, Julian Carr, Desiree Acholla, Colleen Borst, Jessica Johnston, Jennifer Hurst, Melissa Kessler, Elizabeth O'Mara, Tracy Reiman, Liesel Wolff, Kim DeWester, Travis Poland, Laura Frisk, Kaci Fairbanks, Jenny Woods, Allison Liu, Jessica Jagmin, Carrie Ann Knauss, Katie Smith, Kim Terepka, Anita DeWester, Jessica Roland, Madalyn Grimm, Ashley Byrne, and Libby Simons. For

x

the revised cookbook: Neel Parekh, Grace Woodward, Casey Redd, Diana Mendoza, Victoria Hong, Lily Trahan, Kim Johnson, Brittany Hultstrom, Danielli Marzouca, and Alanna Wagy. A special thank you to Scott Brewer for all of his patience and support while listening to Marta chatter on endlessly about recipes. To Erin Nevius, Sara Appino, and Carrie Gellin at Sourcebooks, Inc., for their help on the first edition of this book, and a big thank-you to Michelle Lecuyer and Grace Menary-Winefield for all their help in making this revision a reality!

Finally, a big thank-you to Ingrid E. Newkirk for trusting us with this project, writing a rockin' foreword, and submitting many, many recipes.

PART
ONE

· · · · · · · ·

What You Need to Know

IN THE BEGINNING, THERE WAS THE MICROWAVE

YOU MAY BE WONDERING WHY WE DIDN'T JUST MAKE a vegan cookbook that requires a, you know, stove. Well, we know you're busy. After spending hours on end cramming Shakespeare into your head, we're positive that the last thing you want to do is stand in front of a hot stove stirring sauce or waiting for a pot of water to boil. And c'mon—a microwave is so much more accessible than a stove. Microwave in the student union or your dorm room? Check. Stovetop? Not so much.

Microwaved vegan food. Yum! Okay, we're not totally naive here— we know this probably conjures up an image of a bowl of nuked, wilted kale or some other oh-so-healthy (but possibly gag-inducing) green food. However, at PETA we're all about breaking stereotypes, so we've created a cookbook dedicated to vegan food that doesn't require a stove *and* tastes delicious.

College is supposed to be the time in your life when you're really figuring out how to fend for yourself. You're already trying to figure out physics and how to get out of going to your 8:00 a.m. class, so who has time to learn how to flambé or frappé? Did you know you can actually make pasta without a pot or pancakes without a pan? Well, believe it, buddy. We can teach you all you need to know to make simple, effortless meals. You'll have plenty of time later on in life to make friends with your stove.

We're betting you've been there—nuking package after package of ramen. Opening the freezer with your fingers crossed, hoping there's a frozen burrito lurking behind the ice tray. Or gagging down some pizza, trying your hardest not to dwell on the fact that mold makes interesting shapes in a week—anything to put off actually spending time and effort cooking a meal.

That's where we come in.

Why didn't we make a cookbook that's just like every other one out there? Because we love being the black sheep, the lone wolf, the creep in the back corner. Okay, maybe not that last one, but you get the idea. We dare to be different, and we bet you are itchin' to do the same.

• • • • HEADS UP • • • •

So we know you are old enough and smart enough to know how to work a microwave safely, but we still worry! Please humor us and keep the following in mind when using a microwave:

- Take extreme caution when removing containers of hot food and boiling water from the microwave to avoid spills and burns. Burns don't feel so hot. (Get it?)
- Although most plastic containers are microwave safe, please double-check before putting one in the microwave. When in doubt, use a container that is clearly marked "Microwave Safe" or "Microwavable."
- Of course, no metal objects in the microwave! You know you don't want to be that guy—the person in your dorm or apartment who catches the only working microwave on fire.

Also, FYI, all of these recipes were tested in seven-hundred-watt microwaves and heated on the HIGH setting unless otherwise mentioned in the recipe. Cooking times may vary depending on altitude and microwave.

OK, that should cover all of the boring, lecture-y stuff. On to the fun part!

SHOW US YOUR FOOD!

We know you're gonna take, like, fifteen Instagram shots of your Pancake in a Mug to get the perfect pic to impress all your friends—no filter necessary. We want to see your pics! Follow peta2 on all the sites below and tag us in your food pics from this cookbook along with #PETAsVeganCollegeCookbook.

Instagram and Snapchat: @officialpeta2

Facebook and Twitter: @peta2

FAKIN' IT

FAKE. IT'S NOT EXACTLY THE WORD EVERYONE IS dying for people to call them, we know. But if you can pull off some delicious, satisfying vegan cooking, you've learned to fake your way into people's stomachs quite well. And if you can get all those crazy "omnis" (which is much nicer than calling them "meatheads") you love to devour fakin' bacon, faux riblets, and dairy-free cheese, we'd say you've learned to fake it for animals quite well too. No small feat.

That's what we're helping you to achieve with this cookbook. Fake it until you make it, right? You may turn out to be an award-winning chef someday, but until you become a master of culinary arts, these recipes will get you through. To summarize, this cookbook will put Betty Crocker to shame and do so in a fraction of the time Ms. Crocker spent making her… uh…cheesecakes that are in the freezer section of the grocery store?

We've definitely had our share of culinary catastrophes over the years (we thought smoke alarms were meant to go off while you're making toast), so we wanted to let you lucky readers in on our tricks of the trade. And, no, we're not going to make you go searching for spelt flour or agar-agar. We'll keep things easy for ya.

What about the days your friends want to meet up in the dining hall for lunch? What's a vegan to do then? Well, we're pretty lucky. These days, colleges across the country are more and more vegan friendly, serving up delicious options like vegan pizza, veggie burritos, and even vegan cheese-cake! Many colleges have all-vegan dining stations, and heck, some even have all-vegan dining halls on campus. It's a glorious time to be vegan, my friends. Check out how your school stacks up with other colleges on peta2's Vegan Report Card: VeganReportCard.com.

What if your college doesn't have great vegan food yet? You can change that! We've got your back. Hit us up at peta2@peta2.com and we'll help get you started.

VEGANS—WHAT CAN YOU EAT?

BACK IN THE DAY, THERE WAS THIS STEREOTYPE THAT vegans only ate twigs or berries or lettuce or rocks or…well, you get the point. By the end of this cookbook, that stereotype will just be the punch line to a really bad joke. If you're wondering if vegans can eat this thing or that thing, ask yourself this simple question: Did it come from someone with a pulse? If the answer is yes, well then, it's not vegan. Hot dogs? Had a pulse. Chicken strips? Had a pulse. Glass of milk? Came from someone with a pulse. We have a problem with eating someone or something that came from someone who could stare back at us at one point (except for potatoes…mmm. Stare on, taters!).

Seriously, there's a vegan alternative for almost everything out there. The options available these days are amazing, and we fully recommend taking advantage of them. You can enjoy a veggie dog at a ballpark, throw some vegan chicken patties on the grill at a BBQ, and grab a pint of your favorite dairy-free ice cream from your local grocery store. The possibilities are endless! Get started on your gluttonous cooking journey right now.

STOCK YOUR KITCHEN

YOUR LOCAL DOLLAR STORE HAS TONS OF STAPLES that'll help you get your kitchen necessities together on the cheap—seriously, you'll be amazed at how many of the ingredients needed for the recipes in this book you can find at the dollar store! So look under your bed or in the cushions of the communal couch for some spare change (you might want to wear gloves—you never know what you may find in there) and get the following for a buck each:

* Spices: salt, pepper, garlic powder, onion powder, garlic salt, oregano, Italian seasoning, parsley, granulated onion, chili powder, cumin, basil, rosemary, paprika, seasoning salt, cinnamon, etc.
* Large glass dishes perfect for microwaving soups and pastas
* Storage containers
* Foil, plastic wrap, resealable bags, etc.
* Vinegars: plain, balsamic, and red wine

FIVE ESSENTIALS TO KEEP ON HAND

These products pop up throughout the cookbook, don't require refrigeration, and last what seems like forever. Keep 'em handy!

* Sriracha Hot Chili Sauce
* Ener-G Egg Replacer
* Nutritional yeast
* Minute Rice
* Soy sauce

- Oils: olive and canola
- Flour
- Baking soda
- Sugar: white, brown, and powdered
- Cake mixes and frosting (many store-bought cake mixes and frostings are accidentally vegan, so check the label!)
- Pancake syrup
- Jelly
- Apricot preserves
- Peanut butter
- Breads: veggie dog buns, burger buns, bagels, and bread
- Lime and lemon juice
- Condiments: ketchup, mustard, spicy brown mustard, BBQ sauce, soy sauce, hot sauce, red chili sauce, etc.
- Dried fruits: raisins, cranberries, etc.
- Canned fruits: pineapple, pears, mango, mandarin oranges, apricots, etc.
- Frozen fruits
- Applesauce
- Frozen orange juice concentrate
- Lemonade
- Coconut milk
- Canned veggies: peas, carrots, corn, green beans, beets, asparagus, mushrooms, mixed veggies, etc.
- Sauerkraut
- Jarred artichoke hearts
- Jarred sliced jalapenos
- Olives: black (sliced and whole) and green
- Hummus

* Crackers
* Pretzels
* Tortillas: flour and corn
* Chips: tortilla, potato, and corn
* Nuts: peanuts, almonds, etc.
* Ice
* Popcorn
* Seaweed snacks
* Flatware and utensils
* Dish towels
* Oven mitts
* Pasta
* Pasta sauce
* Salad dressing: a lot of Italian dressings are vegan!
* Ramen
* Tea
* Cereal (they usually have generic brands for Cheerios, Rice Krispies, Fruit Loops, and such)
* Instant oatmeal
* Salsa
* Vegetarian refried beans
* Enchilada sauces: red and green
* Taco shells
* Tomato products: diced tomatoes and green chiles, tomato sauce, tomato paste, tomato soup, etc.
* Taco seasoning (check the ingredients—some contain milk)

FIVE ACCIDENTALLY VEGAN PRODUCTS TO KNOW AND ♥

Some of the recipes in this cookbook call for products like vegan bacon bits and chocolate chips. Here are some brands that make accidentally vegan versions!

• Betty Crocker Bac~Os (Bits and Chips)
• Betty Crocker Bisquick Original
• Nabisco Grahams Original
• Old El Paso Taco Seasoning
• Ghirardelli Semisweet Chocolate Chips

* Manwich sauce (check the label, since not all the Manwich sauces are vegan)
* Pickles
* Relish: dill and sweet
* Canned beans: chickpeas, baked, chili, pinto, black, kidney, etc.
* Rice
* Instant mashed potatoes (check label to make sure they're vegan)
* Minced garlic
* Vegan bacon bits
* Sun-dried tomatoes
* Instant pudding mix
* Paper towels and napkins

SAVE SOME $ AND TIME

The salad bar at your school's dining hall (or at the local grocery store) is awesome for scoring some diced veggies, fruits, or beans for a recipe. It's perfect for when you don't need an entire veggie, or let's be honest—it's also great if you're just feeling lazy. Hit up the salad bar for cucumbers, bell peppers, carrots, broccoli, greens, onions, chickpeas, kidney beans, and more!

The bottom line—maybe you've been vegan for years, maybe you've just gone vegan, or maybe you're looking for a quick way to feed yourself or a reason to hit on the vegan in your psych class. Whatever your motive, we hope you'll enjoy this cookbook. It'll make your life just a bit simpler, so you can, you know, graduate from college and all that. We care about you, after all. We know, we know: we're so thoughtful. Compliment us later—now it's time to get your grub on!

VEGAN ALTERNATIVES TO MEAT, EGGS, AND MILK

THESE DAYS, THERE ARE VEGAN PRODUCTS AND companies popping up everywhere! It's hard to keep track of them all (but fun to try!), so to help you stay on top of it, we put together a list of our fave vegan products and brands. For most of the companies listed below, you can find their products in your local chain grocery store, but some of the products will be easier to find at Whole Foods and health food stores. You can also order many of the products below from websites like VeganEssentials.com.

NOTE:

. . . .

Please check the ingredients of the items you buy to make sure they're vegan; sometimes companies change their ingredients. Often, manufacturers put whey, milk fat, etc., in breads, cereals, and other products. For a list of ingredients you should look out for, please email peta2@peta2.com. At the time of this printing, all the products listed below are vegan.

* **Amy's Kitchen**
  Not an all-vegan company, but it has a ton of delicious vegan options, including frozen pizzas, burritos, veggie burgers, soups (including no-chicken noodle soup), mac 'n'

cheese, chili, enchiladas, and more! Check to make sure it says vegan on the label.
@AMYSKITCHEN

Beyond Meat
Chicken strips, breaded chicken tenders, beefless crumbles, meatballs, burgers, and sliders. One of our faves!
@BEYONDMEAT

Boca
The classic veggie burger (Original Vegan), chik'n patties (Original and Spicy), and ground crumbles.
FACEBOOK.COM/BOCABURGER

Califia Farms
Nondairy milks, coffee creamers, almond milk–based cold brew coffees (including mocha), and seasonally, it offers an awesome almond milk–based pumpkin spice latte!
@CALIFIAFARMS

Daiya
Cheese shreds (cheddar, mozzarella, and pepper jack), cheese slices (cheddar, swiss, and provolone), cheese blocks (cheddar, jalapeño Havarti, jack, and smoked gouda), frozen cheesecakes (New York style, chocolate, strawberry, and key lime), Cheezy Mac, frozen pizzas, cream cheese, and more!
@DAIYAFOODS

❋ **Earth Balance**

So many great vegan products! Try its margarine, cheddar squares (vegan Cheez-Its, anyone?!), aged white cheddar popcorn and puffs, kettle chips (including cheddar and sour cream and onion flavors), and mac 'n' cheese (both cheddar and white cheddar varieties!).
@EARTH_BALANCE

❋ **Ener-G Egg Replacer**

You guessed it: the company makes a great egg replacer for baking!
ENER-G.COM

❋ **Field Roast**

Lots of great vegan meats and cheeses, including deli slices, frankfurters, sausage links (Italian, Mexican chipotle, and smoked apple sage flavors), meatloaf, and breakfast sausage. It also makes some of our fave Thanksgiving staples: celebration roast and hazelnut cranberry roast en croute! And don't miss trying its vegan cheese slices—chao slices.
@FIELDROAST

❋ **Follow Your Heart**

You gotta try its Vegenaise (vegan mayo); cheese slices, blocks, and shreds (flavors include American, provolone, mozzarella, garden herb, parmesan, and Monterey jack); cream cheese; sour cream; and tartar sauce. Don't miss its vegan ranch, bleu cheese, and Caesar dressings—and the VeganEgg!
@FOLLOWYOURHEART

Gardein

Wow, where do we begin? Endless vegan meats—be sure to check out your freezer aisle! Some of our faves include crispy chick'n tenders, chick'n scallopini, barbecue wings, sweet and sour porkless bites, chipotle black bean burger, beefless ground, meatless meatballs, breakfast patties, beefless tips, meatless meatloaf, fishless filet, mini crispy crabless cakes, lightly breaded turk'y cutlet, beefless burger, and a variety of sliders (including beefless and chick'n).
@GARDEIN

GO Veggie!

Makes vegan cheese slices and shreds, as well as grated parmesan topping. But beware: not all of its products are vegan, so be sure to check the label.
@GOVEGGIEFOODS

Hampton Creek

Try its mayonnaise (Just Mayo), cookie dough, and pancake mix.
@HAMPTONCREEK

Lightlife

Lightlife has a ton of great options—everything from veggie dogs to vegan sausage and bacon, chick'n strips, pepperoni, deli slices, tempeh, chorizo sausage, and more!
@LIGHTLIFEFOODS

❋ **Morningstar Farms**

Many of Morningstar's products aren't vegan, but it does have some great options! Don't miss its Hickory BBQ Riblets. Several of its burgers are vegan too.

MORNINGSTARFARMS.COM

❋ **Phoney Baloney's**

Coconut bacon in various flavors.

@PHONEYBALONEYS

❋ **Silk**

Nondairy milks, nondairy milk singles (dark chocolate almond milk is perfect on the go!), yogurt, and creamers. Don't miss its seasonal fave: Silk Nog!

@LOVEMYSILK

❋ **So Delicious**

Nondairy milks, creamers, yogurt, and tons of delicious ice creams (including some awesome cashew-based ice creams in flavors like dark chocolate truffle and salted caramel cluster).

@SO_DELICIOUS

❋ **Sophie's Kitchen**

Vegan tuna, crab cakes, breaded scallops, breaded fishless fillets, breaded shrimp, breaded fishless sticks, breaded coconut shrimp, and smoked salmon.

FACEBOOK.COM/SOPHIES.KITCHEN.VEGAN.PRODUCTS

Sweet Earth Natural Foods

Veggie burgers, frozen burritos (be careful though: not all are vegan), beefless grounds, benevolent bacon, and seitan (in various flavors, including chipotle and curry).

FACEBOOK.COM/SWEETEARTHFOODS

Tofurky

Tofurky makes lots of delicious products: deli slices, sausages, frozen pizzas, pockets, pot pie, chorizo, breakfast links, and our personal faves—tofurky roasts with gravy, perfect for the holidays!

FACEBOOK.COM/TOFURKYFAN

Tofutti

We ♥ its cream cheese, sour cream, Tofutti cuties, and other ice cream treats!

@TOFUTTIBRAND

Upton's Naturals

Upton's has all of your seitan needs covered—everything from bacon seitan strips and ground seitan to chicken seitan. And it has a few jackfruit products too—like Bar-B-Que Jackfruit.

@UPTONSNATURALS

Yves Veggie Cuisine

Veggie dogs, vegan deli slices (ham, turkey, salami, bologna, and roast beef), pepperoni slices, meatless breakfast patties, and Canadian bacon.

FACEBOOK.COM/YVESVEGGIEPAGE

PART
TWO

· · · · · · · · ·

Recipes You'll Love

BREAKFAST

YOU KNOW WHAT THEY SAY. "BREAKFAST IS THE MOST important meal of the day." Hell yeah! How else are you going to motivate yourself to stop hitting the snooze button and get moving for those early classes? And forget those grease-filled breakfasts that just make you more tired. These recipes will keep your energized and full, at least until the dining hall opens for lunch. There's nothing more embarrassing than hearing your stomach growl echoing throughout a lecture hall, but don't worry, we've got you covered. The best thing about these recipes is that you can enjoy them whenever you're in need of a little breakfasty goodness—whether the sun's just coming up or about to go down.

DID YOU KNOW?

Eggs are one of the worst things you can eat. A 2010 Canadian study found that one egg contains three times the cholesterol of a Big Mac. Your body makes all the cholesterol it needs, so consuming any animal protein is going to add bad cholesterol. Plus, eggs are technically a chicken's period—gross!

SMOOTHIE BREAKFAST BOWL

Fresh and oh so fancy. So, grab a spork and
dig in to this healthy highbrow hybrid.

MAKES 1 SERVING

- 1 frozen banana (peeled and cut into chunks before you freeze)
- 1 cup fresh berries, or more if desired
- ½ to ¾ cup almond or soy milk
- ¼ cup vegan granola (optional)

Place the frozen banana, fresh berries, and milk into a blender and blend until smooth. Pour the mixture into a bowl. Slice up more of your berries and sprinkle on top of your smoothie bowl along with granola.

BREAKFAST
PAR-TAY PARFAIT

Perfect for those days when you can't tell
where last night ended and today began.

=== MAKES 1 SERVING ===

- ½ cup granola
- 1 (6-ounce) container vegan yogurt
  (vanilla or fruit flavored)
- 1 banana, sliced
- ¼ cup strawberries or raspberries, sliced

In a tall glass, layer all the ingredients—sand-art style.

MEDITERRANEAN MUESLI

Hard to pronounce but easy to make. Give it a shot!

================= MAKES 1 SERVING =================

- 1 cup rolled oats
- 1 cup vanilla soy milk or rice milk
- 1 cup plain vegan yogurt
- 3 tablespoons dried apricots, chopped
- 3 tablespoons dates, chopped
- Fresh berries (optional)

Mix all the ingredients together in a large bowl and refrigerate for 2 hours. Top with your fave type of berries.

PANCAKE IN A MUG

These tasty babies can be made in a mug, cup, bowl, or whatever you have lying around. Except red plastic Solo cups. 'Cuz they melt, and no one wants Ping-Pong balls in their pancakes.

— MAKES 1 SERVING —

- ½ cup vegan pancake mix
- ¼ cup original or vanilla soy or almond milk
- 2 heaping tablespoons applesauce
- 2 tablespoons frozen blueberries or vegan chocolate chips
- Maple syrup, to taste (optional)
- Vegan margarine, to taste (optional)

In a mug, mix the first four ingredients together, then microwave for 1 to 2 minutes until completely cooked. Top with margarine and maple syrup. Devour!

BREAKFAST NACHOS

Buenas tardes, sunshine. Hitting the snooze button
for the third time didn't work out too well, huh?
Make these nachos delicioso, then take a siesta.

MAKES 3 SERVINGS

- 1 (14-ounce) package firm tofu, drained and rinsed
- 2 cups salsa
- 1 teaspoon onion powder
- 1 (12-ounce) bag tortilla chips
- Sliced avocado or guacamole (optional)
- 3 tablespoons vegan bacon bits (optional)

Mash the tofu in a bowl and microwave for 2 to 3 minutes. Add the salsa and onion powder and stir to blend in with tofu. Nuke for another 30 seconds to a minute until salsa is heated through. Pour chips onto a few different plates and then top the chips with the tofu mixture. Top it off with the avocado/guacamole and bacon bits.

NOTE:

Turn this into a tasty breakfast burrito: chop up a few hash brown patties and vegan breakfast patties and throw everything into a few flour tortillas with the tofu scramble above, and you're good to go!

TOO-LATE-TO-GO-TO-THE-CAF TOFU MASH

Missed the breakfast hours at the dining
hall? Never fear—tofu is here!

MAKES 3 SERVINGS

- 1 (14-ounce) package extra-firm tofu, drained and crumbled
- 1 (7-ounce) can chopped tomatoes, drained
- ¼ cup shredded vegan cheddar cheese
- 1 tablespoon mustard
- 2 teaspoons soy sauce
- Salt and pepper, to taste

Mix everything together in a bowl and nuke for 2 minutes.

FRESHMAN FRITTATA

So easy, a freshman could make it! Just kidding...

MAKES 2 SERVINGS

- 2 cups frozen hash brown potatoes
- ½ cup shredded carrot
- 2 tablespoons vegan margarine
- 1 teaspoon onion powder
- Salt and pepper, to taste
- ¼ cup egg replacer mixed with 1 cup water
- ½ cup original soy milk
- 1 teaspoon mustard
- 1 dash hot sauce
- 1 cup vegan bacon bits
- ½ cup shredded vegan cheddar cheese

In a large bowl, mix together the hash browns, carrots, margarine, and onion powder. Cover and nuke for 5 minutes, stirring once or twice. Season with salt and pepper. In another bowl, mix together the egg replacer, soy milk, mustard, and hot sauce. Stir in the bacon bits and pour the egg-replacer mixture over the hash brown mixture. Stir everything together. Cover and nuke for 3 minutes. Give it a good stir, then nuke for another 5 minutes. If your microwave does not have a turntable, rotate the dish two or three times during the cooking process. Sprinkle the cheese on top, cover, and microwave for another minute, or until the cheese has melted.

FRUIT SKEWER WITH YOGURT SAUCE

Because all food should be on a stick.

MAKES 1 SERVING

- ½ cup strawberry vegan yogurt
- 2 teaspoons lemon juice
- 1 teaspoon agave nectar (you can find it at your local grocery store near the honey)
- ¼ teaspoon nutmeg, grated
- 1 (16-ounce) plastic tub of precut fruit of your choice
- 4 wooden skewers

Combine the yogurt, lemon juice, agave nectar, and nutmeg. Set aside. Thread the fruit on the skewers. Serve with the yogurt sauce for dipping.

GREEK NOMELET

Go Greek without the bothersome pledging
(or the yolks) with our egg-free "omelet."

MAKES 1 SERVING

- 1 cup vegan pancake mix
- ½ cup soy milk
- 1 ½ teaspoons egg replacer mixed
  with 2 tablespoons water
- ¼ cup tofu, drained and cubed
- 8 to 10 Kalamata olives, pitted
- ¼ cup frozen spinach, thawed
- 1 teaspoon garlic powder

In a small bowl, mix together the pancake mix, soy milk, and egg-replacer mixture. Stir until blended. Add the tofu, olives, spinach, and garlic powder. Microwave for 2 minutes or until solid.

TOASTY SAUSAGE SURPRISE

The surprise? Your omni friends will never know this isn't real sausage.

——— MAKES 3 SERVINGS ———

- 1 (14-ounce) tube vegan sausage, crumbled
- 2 cups original soy milk
- 2 tablespoons vegan margarine
- Salt and pepper, to taste
- ¼ cup flour
- 6 slices of bread, toasted

Mix together the sausage, soy milk, margarine, and salt and pepper in a bowl. Microwave for 3 minutes, then add a dash of flour while stirring. Heat for an additional 2 minutes. Repeat this flour-adding process until the mixture is thick. Place toast on plates and top with the sausage mixture.

CRUMB BUM BREAKFAST COBBLER

A nutritious fruit-filled breakfast—crumbs and all.

MAKES 4 SERVINGS

- 1 (16-ounce) can sliced peaches, drained
- 1 (15-ounce) can pear halves, drained and sliced
- ⅓ cup orange juice (optional)
- 1 ½ cups low-fat granola cereal

Place the peaches, pears, and orange juice in a bowl and top with the granola. Nuke for 5 minutes, then remove from the microwave and let stand for 2 minutes before serving.

THE MORNING-AFTER SCRAMBLE

After you're done scrambling to figure out what, exactly, *in the hell you did last night*, whip up a batch of this eggless scramble, sit down, and try to remember where you were and why you're missing a shoe.

MAKES 2 SERVINGS

- ¾ cup salsa
- 1 (14-ounce) package extra-firm tofu, mashed
- Salt, pepper, and garlic powder, to taste
- ⅓ cup original soy milk
- ¼ cup nutritional yeast

Drain most of the liquid from the salsa, mix in a bowl with the tofu, and nuke for about 1 minute or until heated through. Add salt, pepper, and garlic powder. Mix the soy milk and nutritional yeast together in a cup until thick and creamy, then add to the tofu mixture. Nuke for about 2 minutes or until hot, stopping and stirring halfway through. Eat with toast, potatoes, or any vegan meat.

ENGLISH BREAKFAST SANDWICHES

The best brekkie you'll ever have at uni.

—————— MAKES 2 SERVINGS ——————

- ¼ (14-ounce) package extra-firm tofu, drained and mashed
- 1 tablespoon nutritional yeast
- Salt, pepper, and garlic powder, to taste
- 2 vegan breakfast patties (try Gardein or Yves)
- Maple syrup, to taste
- 2 vegan English muffins, toasted
- 2 slices vegan cheddar cheese
- 1 tablespoon sriracha mayo (optional—check out the recipe on page 140)

Mix the tofu, nutritional yeast, salt, pepper, and garlic powder in a small bowl. Nuke for 1 to 2 minutes, until hot. Place the breakfast patties on a plate and nuke according to directions on package. Pour the desired amount of maple syrup onto the patties. Now it's time to assemble the sandwiches! Put the bottom half of one of the English muffins on a plate, then top with one of the breakfast patties, half of the tofu mixture, a slice of the cheese, and the sriracha mayo or a little more maple syrup, and the other half of the English muffin. Nuke the sandwich for 1 minute. Repeat to make the other sandwich.

BUTT-UGLY STICKY BUNS

When plated, they look like a bunch of muddy guys mooning you, but try not to let that turn you off. They're delicious, we promise.

MAKES 8 SERVINGS

- ⅓ cup firmly packed dark brown sugar
- 3 tablespoons vegan margarine
- 1 tablespoon water
- ⅓ cup chopped nuts (optional)
- 1 (8-ounce) can refrigerated vegan biscuits or crescent rounds

Combine the brown sugar, margarine, and water in an 8-inch round microwave-safe dish. Nuke, uncovered, for 2 minutes or until the margarine melts. Stir, then spread evenly across the bottom of the dish. Sprinkle with nuts and then place the biscuits on top. Nuke on medium heat for 4 to 5 minutes, or until the biscuits are firm and no longer doughy. Let stand for 2 minutes, then dump upside down onto a plate.

NOT-JUST-FOR-HIPPIES GRANOLA

You don't have to be crunchy to like
this crunchy breakfast!

━━ MAKES 1 SERVING ━━

- 1 (6-ounce) container vegan yogurt (your fave flavor)
- ½ cup vegan granola
- 3 tablespoons raisins or chopped dates (optional)
- 1 tablespoon almonds or nut of choice (optional)

Mix everything together and eat.

BRAINY BAC'N CHEESE TOAST

Start your morning—okay, afternoon—off right with a gooey breakfast that'll keep you going through that three o'clock class.

───── MAKES 2 SERVINGS ─────

- 2 slices bread, toasted
- 8 cherry tomatoes, halved
- ¼ cup vegan bacon bits
- ½ cup shredded vegan cheddar cheese

Top one slice of bread with half the tomatoes, bacon bits, and cheese. Microwave for 2 minutes or until cheese is melted. Repeat with the remaining slice of bread.

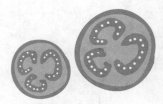

SUNDAY MORNING SAUSAGE IN A BLANKET

When Saturday night has left you semiconscious, barely able to stand, and unable to even use a can opener, quietly put together these easy ingredients, eat, enjoy, and then crawl back under the covers.

MAKES 4 SERVINGS

- 2 vegan sausages
- 1 (8-ounce) can vegan crescent rolls

Cut each sausage in half and then cut each half lengthwise. Wrap the crescent dough around each piece. Pop in the microwave for 10 minutes or until the dough is fluffy.

BROKE-ASS CINNAMON ROLLS

Flat broke? Make your dough go further with this cheap and tasty pastry.

MAKES 1 SERVING

- 1 slice white bread
- Vegan margarine, to taste
- Cinnamon, to taste
- Sugar, to taste

Cut the crust off the bread. Flatten the bread with a can or a rolling pin and spread the margarine on top. Sprinkle with cinnamon and sugar. Roll up like a burrito and cut into minirolls (or just leave it as a burrito if that sounds good or you're in a hurry). Microwave for 15 seconds or until margarine is melted.

AWESOMELY EASY AVOCADO TOAST

Quick and easy to make, so you can get back
to more important things—like jumping back
into that Twitter feud you've got going.

MAKES 2 SERVINGS

- 1 avocado
- 2 slices bread, toasted
- Salt, pepper, and red pepper flakes, to taste

Cut the avocado in half, remove the pit, and scoop out the flesh.
Spread/mash half the avocado onto one slice of the toast, then
repeat for the second slice. Season with salt, pepper, and red
pepper flakes.

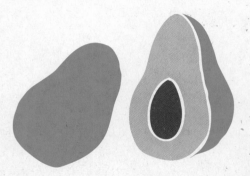

#HASHTAG HASH BROWN CASSEROLE

#handlingmyhashbrowns #veganeats
#NomNomNom #blessed

— MAKES 4 SERVINGS —

- ½ cup nutritional yeast
- ½ cup original soy milk
- 1 tablespoon olive oil
- 1 teaspoon garlic powder
- Salt and pepper, to taste
- 1 (20-ounce) bag shredded potatoes (can also use hash-brown-style potatoes), thawed
- 1 (12-ounce) bag veggie burger crumbles, thawed
- 1 (10-ounce) bag frozen broccoli florets, thawed
- Hot sauce (optional)

Mix the nutritional yeast, soy milk, olive oil, garlic powder, salt, and pepper together to create the cheesy sauce. Set aside. Take a microwave-safe container, lightly coat it with olive oil, and layer the potatoes on the bottom. Add the crumbles and top with the broccoli, cheese sauce, and hot sauce. Microwave on high for 5 minutes or until everything is hot.

SANDWICHES

SANDWICHES ARE THE MOST AMAZING FOOD IN THE world. That's a fact, not opinion. Seriously, who doesn't like sandwiches? They're customizable, portable, filling, and yummy—not to mention easy to make. Whether you like to pile on the vegan meat, load up on veggies, smother your bread with hummus, or tackle all three at once, we've got the sandwich for you. And if you want to make one for us while you're at it, well, let's just say we wouldn't hate you for it.

NOTE:

A lot of breads are vegan, but not all are, so be sure to check the ingredients before you buy!

DID YOU KNOW?

Cows have best friends. Dolphins have names for each other. Pigs are just as intelligent—if not more intelligent—than your dog. Before chicks hatch, they can communicate with each other and their mother through sound. Studies show goats, like us, have accents. Worms communicate by snuggling. Rats laugh. Bees know the world is round and can calculate angles.

44

SLOPPY JOELS

Just as "meaty" as the original Joes, except...well, there's no meat.

—————— MAKES 4 SERVINGS ——————

- 1 (15.5-ounce) can sloppy joe sauce*
- 1 (12-ounce) bag veggie burger crumbles
- 4 buns
- Pickle slices (optional)

Combine the sauce and crumbles in a microwave-safe bowl. Nuke for 2 minutes or until hot. Place on the buns along with pickle slices and serve.

---

* Most Manwich sauces are vegan, but check the label, and watch out for anchovies in the Worcestershire sauce in some brands.

LATE-NIGHT SLOPPY MOES

It's been a long day, and you've got at least another hour's worth of studying ahead. Take a short break and get a little messy—you deserve it.

————— MAKES 4 SERVINGS —————

- 1 ½ cups veggie burger crumbles
- 2 ½ cups tomato puree
- 1 (4-ounce) can diced green chiles
- 1 ½ tablespoons mustard
- 1 tablespoon soy sauce
- 1 tablespoon sugar
- 1 teaspoon onion powder
- Pepper, to taste
- 4 buns

Nuke the crumbles in a bowl until warm. Mix in the rest of the ingredients (except the buns) and heat for 3 minutes. Scoop onto the buns and eat.

UPPER-CRUST
FINGER SANDWICHES

When the family visits, serve 'em these sandwiches.
They'll be so impressed by how well you're getting
along on your own, your 'rents might even overlook
that towering heap of dirty clothes in the corner.

MAKES 4 SERVINGS

- 1 (8-ounce) container vegan cream cheese, softened
- 1 tablespoon chives
- ½ loaf sliced, firm white or wheat bread
- 1 cucumber, sliced

Mix the cream cheese with the chives in a bowl. Spread a thin
layer of the cream cheese mixture onto a slice of bread and top
with cucumber slices. Top with another slice of bread and cut
into quarters. Repeat with the rest of the bread, pile the finger
sandwiches onto a plate, cover with plastic wrap, and chill in the
fridge briefly before serving.

NOTE:

*You can make other finger sandwiches by mixing up your fillings. Mix vegan
cream cheese with some Dijon mustard and add some vegan ham slices for
another tasty sandwich!*

CHICK-UN PARM SAMMICH

Warning: sammich may spontaneously disappear
if left unattended with roommate.

MAKES 1 SERVING

- 1 breaded vegan chicken patty (try Boca)
- 2 tablespoons marinara sauce
- 2 slices bread
- 1 slice vegan mozzarella cheese

Microwave the chicken patty according to directions on the box. Once the chicken patty is done, microwave the marinara sauce for 15 seconds or until warm. Place the chicken patty on one slice of bread and top with the marinara sauce and cheese. Add the other slice of bread and eat.

NOTE:

If you're making this to go, wrap it up in foil. It will keep the sammich warm until you're ready to eat!

HIS MAJESTY'S HUMMUS SANDWICH

A hearty, rustic sandwich fit for a king—
or the captain of the football team.

—————— MAKES 1 SERVING ——————

- ½ cup hummus, or to taste (try the avocado hummus on page 213)
- 2 slices thick-crusted sourdough bread
- 1 to 2 leaves lettuce
- 3 to 4 cherry tomatoes, halved

Spread the hummus on both slices of the bread. Place the lettuce and tomatoes on one piece of bread, then top with the other piece.

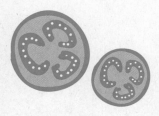

CRAM SANDWICH

Stuff this tasty sandwich in your cake hole so you can go back to stuffing your brain with useless facts and figures.

MAKES 1 SERVING

- 2 tablespoons vegan mayonnaise
- 3 slices bread, toasted
- 6 slices vegan turkey deli slices
- 6 to 8 cherry tomatoes, halved
- 2 tablespoons vegan bacon bits
- 2 large lettuce leaves

Spread mayo on one side of each slice of toast. Place one slice on a plate, mayo side up, and top with half of the turkey, cherry tomatoes, bacon bits, and lettuce. Add another slice of bread, mayo side up, and top with the remaining turkey, tomatoes, bacon bits, and lettuce. Add the third slice of bread, mayo side down this time, and squish the sandwich down so you can eat it!

ASPARA-STUFFED PARM SANDWICH

The fanciest thing you'll ever brown bag to lunch, this savory and satisfying sandwich is guaranteed to get rid of those work-study-slave-wage-job blues in just one bite.

—— MAKES 1 SERVING ——

- ⅓ (10-ounce) package frozen, cut asparagus
- 2 slices bread
- 2 tablespoons vegan mayonnaise
- ½ teaspoon vegan margarine
- 2 teaspoons nutritional yeast
- Pepper, to taste
- 1 to 2 leaves lettuce

Nuke the asparagus until warm, 2 to 3 minutes. Spread one side of each bread slice with 1 tablespoon mayonnaise and ¼ teaspoon margarine. Add some asparagus and sprinkle with nutritional yeast and pepper. Add lettuce and smoosh the two pieces of bread together.

GPA BOOSTER

They say veggies are brain food. Well, if that's true, this tasty wrap is a much smarter way to pass physics than hooking up with your TA.

MAKES 1 SERVING

- 2 tablespoons hummus
- 1 (10-inch) flour tortilla
- ¼ cup shredded lettuce
- 1 tablespoon alfalfa sprouts
- 3 to 4 cherry tomatoes, halved
- Diced cucumbers, to taste
- Salt and pepper, to taste

Spread the hummus on the tortilla. Dump the remaining ingredients onto the wrap, roll up like a burrito, and enjoy!

MEATBALL ANTIHERO

Just like the one you used to get at your
local sub shop, but rest assured, there's no
mystery meat in this hearty version.

─────── MAKES 1 SERVING ───────

- 4 frozen vegan meatless meatballs
- 2 tablespoons marinara sauce
- 1 hoagie roll, split lengthwise
- ⅓ cup shredded vegan mozzarella cheese

Place the meatballs in a microwave-safe dish and heat until hot, about 45 seconds. Remove from the microwave, add the marinara sauce, cover, and return to the microwave. Heat for another 2 minutes or until bubbly. Spoon the meatballs and sauce onto the bread and top with the cheese. Microwave until the cheese melts, about 30 seconds.

NOTE:

If you have a toaster oven, you can skip the microwave and toast the whole mess until the cheese is melted.

SHAM AND CHEEZ

Make your classmates jealous as you roll into class,
homemade sham-and-cheez deliciousness in hand. You'll
have them drooling over vegan food in no time!

―――――――― MAKES 1 SERVING ――――――――

- 1 cup vegan pancake mix
- ½ cup soy or almond milk
- 1 ½ teaspoons Ener-G Egg Replacer
  mixed with 2 tablespoons water
- 4 slices vegan ham, torn into pieces
- ½ cup shredded vegan cheddar cheese
- Mustard, for dipping

In a small bowl, mix together the pancake mix, milk, and egg-replacer mixture. Stir until blended. Add the ham and cheese. Microwave for 2 minutes or until solid. Pry out of the bowl and dip into mustard.

THE HANGOVER "HAM"WICH

Figure out where you're at, find your way home,
vow to never drink again, and fix this easy
breakfast for a late lunch. You're welcome.

——— MAKES 1 SERVING ———

- 4 slices vegan ham
- 2 slices vegan cheddar cheese
- 1 pita, sliced in half

Stuff half the ham and cheese in each side of the pita and nuke for 45 seconds.

"DON'T BE A CHUMP" CHICKPEA SANDWICH

Seriously. You heard us.

MAKES 1 SERVING

- ½ (15-ounce) can of chickpeas, mashed with a fork
- Italian dressing, to taste
- 2 slices bread
- ¼ cup shredded carrots
- 4 cherry tomatoes, halved

Mix the chickpeas with Italian dressing, and spread on one slice of bread. Top with the shredded carrots and tomatoes and then add the other slice of bread.

POULTRYGEIST PITA

Scary good and gone before your eyes.

——— MAKES 1 SERVING ———

- 8 vegan chicken strips
- 1 (8.25-ounce) can mixed vegetables, drained
- 2 tablespoons vegan mayonnaise
- Salt and pepper, to taste
- 1 pita, sliced in half
- 1 to 2 leaves lettuce

Heat the chicken strips in the microwave for 1 minute or until heated through. Tear the chicken strips into pieces. Put in a bowl and add the veggies, mayo, salt, and pepper. Stir together. Stuff in the pita along with some lettuce.

IRON-WILLED GRILLED CHEESE

You're not the kind to let the lack of a stovetop keep you down, no siree. Where there's a will (and an iron), there's a way. Best-tasting food hack ever!

MAKES 1 SERVING

- 1 tablespoon vegan margarine
- 2 slices white bread
- 1 to 2 slices vegan cheddar cheese
- Aluminum foil

Set your iron on the highest setting (usually the linen or cotton setting). While it's heating up, assemble the sandwich: spread the margarine on the top of each slice of bread, then sandwich the cheese between the slices, with the sides with margarine on the outside. Tear off a piece of foil big enough to wrap around the entire sandwich, then wrap the sandwich in the foil. Once the iron is hot, place the iron on the wrapped sandwich and let sit for about 30 seconds. Flip the sandwich over and place the iron on the other side of the sandwich for another 30 seconds. You might need to leave the iron on a few more seconds—take a peek inside and see if the cheese is melted. Eat (and don't forget to turn your iron off!).

RACHEL

Did you know that a vegetarian Reuben sandwich is sometimes called a "Rachel"? It's true. Now that you've learned something new for the day, devour this sandwich.

―――――― MAKES 1 SERVING ――――――

- 4 to 6 slices vegan roast beef–style deli slices (try Tofurky)
- 2 slices whole wheat rye bread, toasted
- 2 slices vegan Swiss cheese
- ¼ cup drained sauerkraut
- 2 tablespoons Thousand-Times-Better Salad Dressing (page 139)

Place the deli slices on the bread and top with the cheese. Nuke until the cheese is melted. Top with the kraut, dressing, and the other slice of bread. Enjoy!

VEGAN CHICK'N CHEEZ STEAK

This yummy, animal-friendly cheez steak is as real as that quote you fudged for your English paper last week, but the deliciousness is oh so real!

MAKES 1 SERVING

- 1 tablespoon vegan mayonnaise
- 1 hoagie roll
- ½ (9-ounce) package vegan chicken strips
- 2 slices vegan provolone cheese
- Salt and pepper, to taste

Spread the mayonnaise on the roll and set aside. Top the chicken strips with the cheese and heat in the microwave until the cheese is melted, about 1 minute. Place on the roll. Sprinkle with salt and pepper and eat.

NOTE:

If you're lucky enough to have a toaster oven, skip the microwave and toast the sandwich until the cheese is nice and melted.

TOFU, OR NOT TOFU, THAT IS THE SANDWICH

Hey, Shakespeare, take a break from pondering existential dilemmas with this yummy sammie that would make even good ol' Will's heart beat in iambic pentameter.

— MAKES 2 SERVINGS —

- ½ (14-ounce) package extra-firm tofu, drained and mashed
- 1 tablespoon relish
- 1 tablespoon roasted sunflower seeds
- 1 tablespoon vegan mayonnaise
- 2 teaspoons mustard
- 2 teaspoons onion powder
- 2 teaspoons soy sauce
- ¼ teaspoon garlic powder
- 4 slices bread, toasted
- 2 leaves lettuce
- 4 cherry tomatoes, halved

Mix the tofu, relish, sunflower seeds, mayonnaise, mustard, onion powder, soy sauce, and garlic powder in a bowl. Spread onto two pieces of toast. Top each with a lettuce leaf and 4 tomato halves, and put the remaining bread on top.

BANGIN' BBQ TOFU

When everything else in your fridge has gone bad, you can always depend on that block o' tofu to be as fresh as the day you bought it two months ago. Seriously, your student ID will expire before that tofu, so enjoy a BBQ sandwich or two and then clean out your fridge.

MAKES 4 SERVINGS

- 1 (14-ounce) package extra-firm tofu, drained and cut in half horizontally
- 1 cup BBQ sauce
- 4 sandwich rolls
- Sandwich fixings (lettuce, tomato, vegan mayo, etc.)

Wrap the tofu slices in paper towels and put on a plate. Top with another plate and place a heavy book on top. Refrigerate for an hour or so. Unwrap the tofu, pat dry, and place in a large bowl. Spoon ¾ cup of the BBQ sauce over the tofu, cover the bowl, and let marinate overnight. The next day, place the tofu on a plate and nuke for 2 minutes. Cut the tofu into thin slices and place on sandwich rolls with the rest of the sandwich fixings. Spoon the BBQ sauce over the sandwich fixings.

SPOTLIGHT ON: PEANUT BUTTER

PEANUT BUTTER IS AN EXTREMELY VERSATILE FOOD—after all, there aren't many foods you can use in a sandwich and a dessert. Well, we guess you could use hummus in a sandwich and a dessert, but we don't recommend it. Peanut butter is a protein-packed, stick-to-the-roof-of-your-mouth, delicious culinary device that we're sure you will love as much as we do. We apologize in advance if you become addicted.

DID YOU KNOW?

You get protein from everything you eat. Plant-based foods that provide high amounts of protein include whole wheat bread, peanut butter, beans, soy, oatmeal, peas, mushrooms, broccoli, and quinoa. Most people in America consume too much protein in a day, which is linked to health issues like heart disease, cancer, obesity, and diabetes.

KNOCK-OATS

Packed with peanutty protein and potassium,
this breakfast of champions is a one-two
punch of health and deliciousness.

MAKES 1 SERVING

- 1 packet instant vegan oatmeal
- 1 banana, sliced thin
- 2 tablespoons peanut butter
- 1 teaspoon cinnamon

Prepare the oatmeal according to the package instructions. While hot, stir in the banana slices, peanut butter, and cinnamon.

WICKED GOOD WAFFLEWICH

Super sweet, this wicked, weird-looking PB-and-chocolate-chip monstrosity is fugly but fabulous.

————— MAKES 1 SERVING —————

- Peanut butter, to taste
- 2 frozen vegan waffles, toasted
- Vegan chocolate chips, to taste
- Maple syrup, to taste

Smear the peanut butter on both waffles and then sprinkle them with the desired amount of chocolate chips. Nuke for about 10 seconds. Smash the waffles together and top it all off with the maple syrup.

APPLE "BREAD" PB SAMMIE

Sure, you could be sweet and make one for your roomie, but nah. She knows what she did.

MAKES 2 SERVINGS

- 1 small or medium apple
- 4 tablespoons peanut butter
- Handful of vegan semisweet chocolate chips (optional)

Cut the apple, width-wise, into four thick rounds, then carefully cut out the core from each apple slice. Spread the peanut butter onto one slice, then sprinkle with the chocolate chips. Top with the other apple slice. Repeat to make the second sandwich.

SUPER QUICKIE PEANUT SAUCE

Like most things this good, no matter how hard you try to make it last, you're done way too soon.

―――――― MAKES 2 SERVINGS ――――――

- 5 tablespoons hot water
- 3 tablespoons peanut butter
- 2 tablespoons soy sauce
- 2 teaspoons lemon juice
- 1 teaspoon chili-garlic sauce

Put all the ingredients in a medium-size bowl and stir until combined. (Add more water if you want a thinner consistency.) Nuke for 30 seconds. Serve over steamed veggies and fried or steamed tofu, or use as a dipping sauce for spring rolls, veggies, and tofu.

BUNNY BUTTER SPREAD

Rabbit food never tasted so good.

MAKES 8 SERVINGS

- ¼ cup grated carrots
- 2 tablespoons chunky peanut butter
- 1 tablespoon orange juice
- 1 tablespoon raisins

Stir all the ingredients together and serve on bread or with crackers.

THAI TAKEOUT
(Hold the Takeout)

Too busy with studying to make it to dinner? Thai-dy up your notes while you nosh on this delish meal in a bowl.

———— MAKES 1 SERVING ————

- 1 cup microwavable rice
- 2 tablespoons peanut butter
- 1 teaspoon soy sauce

Cook the rice according to the directions on the package. Add the peanut butter and soy sauce, making sure that each grain of rice is coated. Mix together and eat!

CHOCOLATEY PB BANANA BINGE BITES

Whip up a batch (or three) and binge watch your
fave TV show until your vision gets blurry.

— MAKES 1 SERVING —

- ¼ cup peanut butter, at room temperature
- 1 banana, sliced into ¼-inch slices
- 1 cup vegan chocolate chips
- 1 tablespoon soy or almond milk
- Toothpicks

Add a dollop of peanut butter to one banana slice, then top with another slice. Stick a toothpick through the center. Repeat the process with the remaining banana slices. Freeze the banana bites until firm—at least 1 hour. Put the chocolate chips and milk into a mug and microwave, stirring every 10 to 15 seconds, until melted and smooth. Remove the banana bites from the freezer and dip each in the melted chocolate to coat. Freeze again until solid—at least 1 hour.

PBR CRISPY TREATS

No, not the cheap beer. You could pair that
with this tasty treat, but we recommend
a tall, frosty glass of almond milk.

——————————— MAKES 12 SQUARES ———————————

- 1 cup light corn syrup
- 1 cup smooth peanut butter
- 1 cup sugar
- 6 cups puffed rice cereal

Grease a 9 × 13-inch pan with vegetable oil. Mix the corn syrup, peanut butter, and sugar in a large, microwavable bowl. Heat slowly until the sugar dissolves, stirring every minute or so—this should just take a few minutes. Remove from the microwave, and stir in the cereal right away. Spread into the pan and chill until firm. Cut and eat!

FINALS WEEK FUDGE

It's tasty, but it won't get you an A on your calculus exam.

———————————— MAKES 10 PIECES ————————————

- ¾ cup vegan margarine
- 1 cup peanut butter
- 1 ¾ cups powdered sugar

Grease a 9 × 9-inch pan with vegan margarine or vegetable oil. Put the margarine in a bowl, and nuke for 30 seconds or until mostly melted. Stir in the peanut butter right away, while the bowl and margarine are still warm. Add the powdered sugar a little bit at a time, mixing well. Pour into the pan and put in the fridge for at least 30 minutes. Cut into squares and serve.

PERFECT PEANUT BUTTER MOUSSE

This is perfection in a PB confection.

— MAKES 4 SERVINGS —

- 1 (12.3-ounce) block lite firm silken tofu
- ½ cup peanut butter (more or less, to taste)
- ½ cup powdered sugar

Blend the tofu, peanut butter, and powdered sugar in a blender until smooth. Transfer to a bowl and refrigerate for an hour before serving.

PB BOMBS

Take one every hour to relieve symptoms of bombed tests. Warning: will not get you through medical school.

MAKES 8 PB BOMBS

- 2 tablespoons vegan margarine
- ½ cup powdered sugar
- 4 vegan graham crackers, crushed into crumbs
- ¼ cup peanut butter

Melt the margarine in the microwave—about 15 to 20 seconds—then mix everything together in a big bowl. Using your hands, roll the dough into golf ball–sized balls. Chill in the fridge before serving. This recipe can easily be doubled or tripled!

FROZEN FRAT BALLS

'Cuz frat boys really need to chill.

— MAKES 24 PIECES —

- 1 (28-ounce) jar creamy peanut butter
- 3 cups powdered sugar
- 1 (12-ounce) bag vegan semisweet chocolate chips

Using your hands (c'mon, it's fun!), thoroughly smoosh the peanut butter and the powdered sugar together in a bowl, forming a dough. Roll 1-inch balls with the dough and place on a cookie sheet that's been covered with parchment or wax paper. Freeze for at least an hour. Remove from the freezer and set aside. Put the chocolate chips in a bowl and nuke for 1 minute. Stir. Heat for another 30 seconds, if necessary, and stir until smooth. Spoon onto the peanut butter balls and freeze for at least an hour. Store in a cool, dry place.

ANTS ON A VLOG

A quick and healthy snack for all you die-hard vloggers too busy trying to become YouTube stars to make a meal.

——— MAKES 1 SERVING ———

- ¼ cup peanut butter
- 2 stalks celery, cut into sticks
- 1 small box raisins

Spread the peanut butter on the celery and top with raisins.

HIPPIE-DIPPIE TRAIL MIX

You may not be a granola kid, but after eating
this amazing snack, you might just enjoy
the scent of patchouli a little more.

— MAKES 4 SERVINGS —

- 1 cup Nature Valley Crunchy peanut butter granola bars, crumbled into small pieces
- 1 cup pretzel sticks, broken in half
- 1 cup raisins
- ½ cup sunflower kernels

Put everything in a gallon-size plastic bag and shake until completely mixed.

MYSTERY BARS

Are they breakfast? Are they dessert? Who cares?

———— MAKES 8 BARS ————

- 7 cups of your fave crunchy vegan cereal
- 1 ½ cups dried fruits
- 1 teaspoon cinnamon
- ¾ cup brown rice syrup or agave nectar
- ¾ cup peanut butter
- 2 tablespoons vegan margarine

Spray a 9 × 13-inch pan with cooking spray. Put the cereal, dried fruits, and cinnamon in a very large bowl and mix together. Put the syrup, peanut butter, and margarine in a large dish and nuke for 45 seconds to 1 minute, until almost melted. Stir till smooth and immediately pour over the cereal mixture, mixing everything together well. Pour into the pan. Freeze for at least 2 hours or overnight. Cut into squares and enjoy!

O BABY BARS

O baby, I want more! And lucky for you,
since they're homemade, you can eat as
many as your little heart desires.

—————— MAKES 12 BARS ——————

- 3 ½ cups O-shaped vegan cereal
- 2 tablespoons vegan chocolate chips, or more if desired
- ½ cup maple syrup
- ½ cup peanut butter

Grease a 9 × 13-inch pan with vegetable oil. Put the cereal and chocolate chips in a large bowl and set aside. Put the maple syrup and peanut butter in a dish, and nuke for about 30 seconds, until almost melted. Stir until smooth and immediately pour over the cereal mixture, stirring until all the cereal is coated. Press into the greased pan and refrigerate for at least 30 minutes. When cool, cut into bars.

PEANUT BUTTER CUP PIE

Chock-full of creamy chocolate and peanut butter, you'll love this vegan Reese's to pieces.

—————— MAKES 8 SERVINGS ——————

- ¾ cup semisweet vegan chocolate chips
- 2 (10.5-ounce) packages firm silken tofu
- ¾ cup peanut butter
- 1 tablespoon maple syrup
- 1 (9-inch) vegan graham cracker piecrust
- 1 ripe banana, thinly sliced

Put the chocolate chips in a microwave-safe bowl, and microwave for 1 minute or until the chips are melted. In a blender, puree the melted chocolate with the tofu, peanut butter, and maple syrup until smooth. Cover the bottom of the piecrust with slices of banana. Pour the tofu mixture over the banana slices and chill for at least 2 hours.

PB&C NO-BAKE COOKIES

Cookies you don't have to slave over
a stove for? Yes, please!

───────── MAKES 14 COOKIES ─────────

- ⅔ cup maple syrup
- ¼ cup cocoa powder
- ¼ cup vegan shortening
- ½ cup peanut butter
- 2 cups rolled oats
- 1 teaspoon cinnamon

Put the syrup, cocoa powder, and shortening in a bowl, and nuke for about 30 seconds. Add the peanut butter and nuke for an additional 45 seconds. Stir right away and continue stirring until combined. Add the oats and cinnamon and stir until well combined. Drop onto wax paper and put in the fridge for at least a half an hour before serving.

WILD OATS
CHOCOLATE COOKIES

Sow your wild oats and reap some kick-ass cookies.

——— MAKES 12 SERVINGS ———

- 2 cups sugar
- ½ cup soy milk
- ½ cup vegan margarine
- ¼ cup cocoa powder
- ½ cup peanut butter
- 3 cups quick oats

Nuke the sugar, soy milk, margarine, and cocoa powder in large bowl on high for 3 minutes. Stir, then nuke for 2 more minutes. Remove from heat. Add the peanut butter and stir until melted. Add oats and stir. Drop spoonfuls onto plates covered with wax paper. Refrigerate until cool.

SALADS

VEGAN MEATS, SESAME SEEDS, RED BEANS, CHICK-peas, marinated tofu, nuts, orange segments—anything goes when it comes to these salads! We make things super-easy for you by letting you in on all the right fixin's to make a ridiculously awesome-looking salad that will get all your friends begging you for a bite. A big bowl of one of these numbers can certainly rock your world!

DID YOU KNOW?

Going vegan can help you lose weight. Taking animal-based foods out of your diet will eliminate cholesterol and greatly reduce the amount of fat and calories you are taking in. Your calorie intake will be replaced with foods like fruits, vegetables, grains, legumes, nuts, and seeds, which all have vital nutrients to make your body and mind the healthiest they can be. Many people go vegan for health issues or weight loss—both are a silver lining to saving animals!

"OPEN A CAN" BEAN SALAD

If you have time to open five cans, well then, your lunch is basically made. You're welcome.

—————— MAKES 4 SERVINGS ——————

- 1 (15.5-ounce) can corn
- 1 (15-ounce) can black beans
- 1 (14.5-ounce) can diced tomatoes (with peppers and onions is best)
- 1 (15-ounce) can black-eyed peas
- 1 (15-ounce) can chickpeas (aka garbanzo beans)
- ½ (8-ounce) bottle Italian dressing
- 1 tablespoon chopped chives

Put the corn and beans in a large colander and rinse well. Drain most of the liquid from the canned tomatoes. Combine all the ingredients in a large bowl. If desired, pour in more Italian dressing, but it shouldn't be soupy. Stir together and serve.

NOTE:
....

This salad is even tastier if you let it sit in the fridge and marinate for a couple of hours. This recipe will make nearly a week's worth of easy lunches.

LEAFY (NOT) NUGGETS

A painless way to get your greens. Kind of like "studying" while watching TV.

MAKES 2 SERVINGS

- 1 (10-ounce) bag salad greens
- 2 breaded vegan chicken patties
- Vegan salad dressing, to taste

Dump the lettuce onto a plate and set aside. Nuke the chicken patties until heated through, about a minute for each patty. Cut up the patties and scatter over the lettuce. Toss with your favorite dressing. Enjoy!

CRAY CRAY CRANBERRY CHICK'N SALAD

A crazy combo of yummy ingredients, this salad is more mixed-up than your ex but a lot healthier for you.

—— MAKES 4 SERVINGS ——

- 1 (9-ounce) bag vegan chicken strips (try Beyond Meat's Lightly Seasoned Strips), thawed and chopped
- ½ cup dried cranberries
- ½ cup vegan mayonnaise
- ¼ cup chopped pecans
- 2 green onions, chopped
- 1 celery stalk, chopped
- ¼ teaspoon dried dill
- Salt and black pepper, to taste

Mix all the ingredients together in a bowl. For the best flavor, refrigerate overnight. Serve on top of lettuce, with crackers, or in a sandwich.

LIP-SMACKIN' THAI VEGGIES

The splash of lime will have you puckering up as much as your serial lip-locking suite mate—no lip balm required.

— MAKES 1 SERVING —

- 2 cups chopped/sliced mixed veggies (e.g., zucchini, bell peppers, onions)
- ½ cup chopped nuts
- Handful of bean sprouts
- 1 tablespoon lime juice
- 1 tablespoon olive oil
- ½ teaspoon salt

Put everything in a huge bowl and toss together. Crunch away!

STRAWBERRY FIELD GREENS FOREVER

Vegan chicken + strawberries = delicious.

MAKES 2 SERVINGS

- 6 vegan chicken strips
- 1 (10-ounce) bag field greens
- ½ cup sliced strawberries
- Italian dressing, to taste

Nuke the chicken strips in the microwave for 1 minute or until heated through. Tear up the chicken and place in a bowl. Add the other ingredients and toss to coat.

RUSH WEEK GREEK SALAD

No pledging necessary.

———— MAKES 2 SERVINGS ————

- 1 (14-ounce) package firm tofu, drained and cut into 1-inch cubes
- Italian dressing, to taste
- 1 cup cucumber slices
- 8 to 10 cherry tomatoes
- ½ cup pitted Kalamata olives
- 1 (10-ounce) bag lettuce (your choice)

Pour the dressing over the tofu in a large bowl and refrigerate for at least 1 hour. Add the cucumbers, tomatoes, and olives, and toss to coat. Serve on the lettuce.

IN A PICKLE
CHICKPEA SALAD

Remember that time you hooked up with your
roommate's ex? This salad is like that—
scandalous, yet it makes you feel oh so good!

MAKES 2 SERVINGS

- 1 (15-ounce) can chickpeas, drained and rinsed
- 1 cup finely chopped celery
- 1 to 2 tablespoons nutritional yeast
- 2 teaspoons onion powder
- Dill pickle relish, to taste
- Salt, to taste
- Vegan mayonnaise, to taste

Mix all the ingredients, except the mayo, together, mashing the chickpeas slightly as you mix. Once it's mixed to a soft, spreadable consistency, add the mayo until the salad is as moist as you like. Eat as is, or use on top of crackers or in a sandwich.

"ROCK OUT WITH YOUR BROC OUT" SALAD

Flaunt those florets!

—————— MAKES 3 TO 4 SERVINGS ——————

- ½ cup vegan mayonnaise
- 2 tablespoons sugar
- ½ tablespoon rice vinegar
- ½ teaspoon onion powder
- 2 ½ cups broccoli florets, chopped into small pieces
- 1 to 2 carrots, chopped into small pieces
- ¼ cup sunflower kernels
- 2 to 3 tablespoons vegan bacon bits

Mix together the mayo, sugar, rice vinegar, and onion powder in a large bowl. Add the broccoli and carrot, and stir to coat. Refrigerate for 1 hour, then add the sunflower kernels and bacon bits and serve.

AVOCADO "KALE CAESAR!" SALAD

Forget the Romaine Empire. All hail
kale in this kick-ass version.

MAKES 1 SERVING

- 3 cups chopped kale
- 1 cup vegan croutons (see recipe on page 247)
- ½ avocado, peeled, pitted, and sliced
- ¼ small red onion, thinly sliced
- Vegan Caesar dressing, to taste (try Follow Your Heart's)

Combine the kale, croutons, avocado, and onion in a large bowl.
Top with the dressing, then toss and serve.

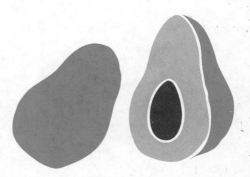

SPICY WATERMELON SALAD

You know what they say: you are what you eat.
This salad will show people that you're not
just sweet; you have a bit of an edge too.

─────── MAKES 2 SERVINGS ───────

- 4 cups cubed watermelon
- 1 large cucumber, peeled and cubed
- ½ (4-ounce) can minced jalapeños
- 2 tablespoons lime juice
- 2 tablespoons white vinegar
- Salt, to taste

Combine all the ingredients in a large bowl. Gently toss to coat.
Chill for at least 1 hour and serve cold.

FRUIT SALAD
ON THE FLY

2 fruits + 2 minutes = 2 delicious 2 share.

─────────────── MAKES 1 SERVING ───────────────

- 1 orange, peeled
- 4 strawberries
- 1 tablespoon lime juice

Cut the orange and the strawberries into bite-size pieces. Put in a bowl. Sprinkle with the lime juice, and stir to combine. Enjoy!

CUKE-CHICK SALAD

Chickpeas and cucumbers make a much better
duo than you and your last lab partner.

—————————— MAKES 2 SERVINGS ——————————

- ½ (15-ounce) can chickpeas
- 2 cucumbers, sliced
- ¼ cup distilled vinegar
- 1 teaspoon onion powder
- Salt and pepper, to taste

Put the chickpeas and cucumbers in a bowl. Add the vinegar and onion powder, and stir everything together. Add salt and pepper as needed.

"GOES BOTH WAYS" CHICK SALAD

All we're saying is that this versatile salad is just as happy in a pita pocket as it is on a bed of lettuce leaves. Get your mind out of the gutter!

— MAKES 2 SERVINGS —

- 1 (8-ounce) package vegan chicken, shredded or diced
- 3 teaspoons dill pickle relish
- 1 cup vegan mayonnaise
- 1 teaspoon black pepper
- 1 teaspoon garlic powder
- Salt, to taste

Mix the chicken and dill pickle relish together in a bowl. Add the mayo and mix. Add the seasonings and mix again. Serve on a salad, in a pita pocket, etc.

EXCLAMATION POINT EGGLESS SALAD!

There are no periods in this salad—*chicken periods, aka eggs. Yeah, we'd rather eat tofu too.*

MAKES 4 SERVINGS

- 1 (14-ounce) package extra-firm tofu, drained
- ½ cup vegan mayo
- ¼ cup relish
- 2 to 3 stalks green onion, chopped
- 1 ½ tablespoons Dijon mustard
- ¼ teaspoon turmeric (for the yellowy color)
- Salt and pepper, to taste
- 8 slices bread
- Lettuce, tomato, and onion (optional)

Mash the tofu with a fork in a large bowl. Add in all the other ingredients (except the bread and optional toppings, of course), and mix well. Once combined, spread some of the mixture on one slice of bread. Add the lettuce, tomato, and onion, then top with the other slice of bread. Repeat until you've used up all of your mixture.

SLICE OF LIFE
CHEF SALAD

Chef salads are usually big plates of dead
things with a little lettuce. We guarantee
that our version is animal free.

—————— MAKES 2 SERVINGS ——————

- 1 (10-ounce) bag salad greens
- ½ cup vegan cheddar cheese, shredded or cubed
- 4 slices vegan ham, torn into pieces
- 2 slices vegan turkey, torn into pieces
- 10 cherry tomatoes, halved
- ¼ cup vegan bacon bits
- Vegan ranch dressing (try the one on page 133) or vegan blue cheese dressing (there's a great one on page 141), to taste

Place all the dry ingredients into a large bowl and toss together. Add the dressing and toss again. Enjoy!

NUKE-LEAR MELTDOWN CHILI TACO SALAD

So named because you nuke it...and it melts. Shut up—this is damn good, and you know it.

MAKES 2 SERVINGS

- 1 (15-ounce) can chili beans in sauce
- 1 (12-ounce) bag veggie burger crumbles
- ¾ cup shredded vegan cheddar cheese
- 1 bag tortilla chips
- 1 cup shredded lettuce
- ½ cup salsa
- Jalapeños, to taste

Put the beans and the veggie burger crumbles in a large bowl. Nuke for 3 minutes. Top with the cheese and nuke for another 30 seconds or until melted. Put some tortilla chips on two plates. Top each plate of chips with half the chili mixture, then top with the lettuce, salsa, and jalapeños.

CORNY SALAD

This salad is corny in the filled-with-corn-
deliciousness kinda sense—not in the embarrassing-
joke-Dad-tells-to-your-friends kinda sense.

————— MAKES 2 SERVINGS —————

- 3 tablespoons olive oil
- 2 teaspoons lime juice
- 1 teaspoon sugar
- ½ teaspoon salt
- ¼ teaspoon pepper
- 2 cups frozen corn, thawed
- 2 cups halved cherry tomatoes
- 1 cup peeled, chopped cucumber

Mix together the olive oil, lime juice, sugar, salt, and pepper in a
large bowl. Add the corn, tomatoes, and cucumber and stir until
fully combined.

FRESH OFF THE "VINE" FRUIT SALAD

Sorry to hear about that Vine going viral. Public humiliation can leave a bad taste in your mouth. Freshen up with some fruity goodness.

MAKES 2 SERVINGS

- 1 (20-ounce) can diced pineapple, drained
- 1 (16-ounce) plastic tub of precut fruit of your choice
- 2 (6-ounce) containers vegan yogurt (your fave flavor)
- ½ bunch of red seedless grapes

Mix together and enjoy!

MIDTERM MACARONI SALAD

Just what you need to keep focused and restore your sanity when your eyes start to blur and you can't stop mumbling about the five hundred pages you have left to read before your midterm tomorrow.

=== MAKES 4 SERVINGS ===

- ½ cup frozen peas
- ½ (16-ounce) box macaroni
- ¾ cup vegan mayonnaise
- 1 heaping teaspoon Dijon mustard
- Salt, to taste
- ½ (10-ounce) bag shredded carrots
- 3 tablespoons chopped chives

Cook the peas according to the package directions and set aside. Put the macaroni in a large microwave-safe container and pour in water until macaroni is completely submerged (about ¾ of the way full). Microwave on high for 5 minutes, stir, and repeat until macaroni is tender, generally about 10 to 12 minutes. While the macaroni is heating up, mix the mayonnaise and mustard together and add salt as needed. Drain all the water from the macaroni and add the carrots, peas, and chives. Top with the mayo/mustard sauce. Mix until well coated and refrigerate until ready to serve.

CHICK FLICK SALAD

Guys, invite your girlfriend over and eat this salad
while watching a rom com, and we guarantee she'll be
all over you like...er...salad dressing on a salad?

MAKES 2 SERVINGS

- 1 (9-ounce) bag vegan chicken strips
- 1 (10-ounce) bag lettuce, your choice
- ½ (10-ounce) bag shredded carrots
- 10 cherry tomatoes
- 2 tablespoons olive oil
- 1 tablespoon lemon juice
- Salt and pepper, to taste

Nuke the chicken for about 2 minutes or until hot. Set aside. Mix all the veggies together in a large bowl and add the olive oil, lemon juice, salt, and pepper. Toss the salad until the veggies are well coated. Top with the chicken and serve.

"LAST CALL" LENTIL AND CARROT SALAD

A healthy meal before a less-than-healthy night out.
Great for your stamina and your eyesight. Warning:
won't help *at all* once you've got your beer goggles on.

MAKES 1 SERVING

- 1 tablespoon red wine vinegar
- 2 teaspoons olive oil
- 2 or 3 squirts of lemon juice
- ¼ teaspoon garlic powder
- 1 (15-ounce) can lentils, rinsed and drained
- 1 large carrot, chopped into small pieces
- ¼ of a small red onion, finely chopped
- Salt and pepper, to taste

Stir together the vinegar, oil, lemon juice, and garlic powder in a medium-size bowl. Mix in the lentils, carrot, and onion, then season with salt and pepper. Stir well and enjoy.

NOTE:

This salad gets better the longer it sits, so this is great to stick in the fridge in a to-go container to take with you for lunch between classes!

FAKIN' BACON 'N' ORANGE SPINACH SALAD

Make a five-star salad in less than 5 minutes.

— MAKES 2 SERVINGS —

- 1 (8-ounce) bag fresh spinach
- 1 orange, peeled and sliced into thin rounds
- 1 tablespoon sesame seeds
- 2 tablespoons rice vinegar
- 1 tablespoon orange juice concentrate
- 1 tablespoon water
- 1 tablespoon vegan bacon bits

Put the spinach leaves in a bowl along with the orange slices. Put the sesame seeds in a blender and grind into a powder. Add the vinegar, orange juice concentrate, and water to the blender, and blend to mix. Pour over the salad and add the bacon bits. Toss before serving.

FIELD OF GREENS

Even easier than falling asleep in statistics.

—— MAKES 2 SERVINGS ——

- ½ (10-ounce) bag salad greens
- 1 (15-ounce) can chickpeas, drained and rinsed
- ½ (10-ounce) bag shredded carrots
- 1 cucumber, peeled and chopped
- ½ cup sunflower seeds

Mix everything together and top with your favorite salad dressing.

BLACK BEAN AND CORN SALAD

If your taste buds wanna dance, here's the extended mix.

MAKES 2 SERVINGS

- 1 (15-ounce) can black beans, drained and rinsed
- 1 (15-ounce) can diced tomatoes with green chiles
- 1 (8.75-ounce) can corn, drained
- ¼ cup balsamic vinegar
- 2 tablespoons vegetable oil
- 1 teaspoon chives
- ½ teaspoon salt
- ½ teaspoon sugar
- ½ teaspoon pepper
- Hot sauce, to taste

Mix all the ingredients together. Chill before serving.

NOTE:

This also makes an excellent dip served with tortilla chips.

SAFFI'S CHICK SALAD

Tabbouleh's grainy friend. Just as refreshing as tabbouleh without being bulgur.

MAKES 2 SERVINGS

- 1 ½ cups instant rice
- ½ (15-ounce) can chickpeas, drained and rinsed
- 1 long English cucumber, peeled and finely chopped
- ⅓ cup lemon juice
- ⅓ cup olive oil
- 4 tablespoons dried parsley
- 1 tablespoon chives
- 1 teaspoon salt
- ½ teaspoon pepper

Cook the rice according to the package directions. Toss everything together in a large bowl and dig in!

DIRTY CHICK (PEA) CLEAN-UP SALAD

You had pizza and beer for every meal over the weekend. Clean up your act with this healthy and satisfying "cleanse" meal.

— MAKES 1 SERVING —

- 1 (15.5-ounce) can chickpeas, drained and rinsed
- 1 red delicious or gala apple, cored and diced
- ¼ cup diced celery
- Salt, to taste

Mix all the ingredients together and serve.

SLAW IN THE RAW

Your parents will be much happier being presented
with this salad instead of that nude charcoal sketch you
posed for in art class when you needed extra cash.

MAKES 2 SERVINGS

- 1 (16-ounce) bag shredded cabbage
- ½ cup lemon juice
- ½ cup roasted sunflower seeds or chopped nuts
- ½ cup vegan mayonnaise
- Salt and pepper, to taste

Place all the ingredients in a large mixing bowl and stir to combine.
Chill for 30 minutes, then serve.

ULTIMATE FRISBEE FRUIT SALAD

Fling together this fruity pick-me-up after
you wash the mud off your face.

MAKES 4 SERVINGS

- 2 apples, cored and cut into quarters
- ½ cup water
- 1 cup peanuts
- ½ cup soy milk
- 2 cups cubed fresh fruit (try pears, cantaloupe, bananas— whatever you like) or 1 (15-ounce) can fruit salad, drained
- Handful of raisins

Blend the apples and ¼ cup of water in a food processor (a blender will do in a pinch—just cut your apples into the smallest pieces possible). Add the peanuts, soy milk, and enough of the remaining water to reach a smooth consistency. Divide the fruit into four bowls and top with the peanut cream mixture. Sprinkle with raisins and serve.

KINESIOLOGY 101 SALAD

You thought you were done with PE in high school.
Boy, were you wrong. At least this salad won't weigh
you down while you're forced to do push-ups.

——— MAKES 2 SERVINGS ———

- 1 (10-ounce) bag salad greens
- ¼ cup chopped walnuts
- ¼ cup shredded cabbage
- ¼ cup shredded carrots
- ¼ cup sliced fresh mushrooms
- Salad dressing, to taste

Combine all the ingredients in a bowl, toss together, and eat!

SOUPS, STEWS, AND CHILIS

A HEARTY SOUP, CHILI, OR STEW CAN COMFORT YOU better than your roomie, your significant other, your toastiest pair of microwaved socks, or even your mom. They leave you satisfied and warm—even if you're alone in your dorm room instead of sitting around the family table back home. Invite a friend over, or your RA, and you can do some old-fashioned bonding over asparagus soup. Everyone does that, right? It's not just us?

——— DID YOU KNOW? ———
One vegan saves more than one hundred animals every single year—just by not eating them!

SPRINGTIME IN ASPARAGUS SOUP

Have you heard that green is the new
black? Well, it's also the new soup.

—————— MAKES 2 SERVINGS ——————

- 1 (10-ounce) package frozen, cut asparagus (you can also use fresh)
- 1 cup veggie broth
- 2 tablespoons vegan margarine
- 2 teaspoons onion powder
- 1 dash garlic powder
- 1 dash pepper
- 1 cup original soy or almond milk

Mix all the ingredients, except the milk, together in a bowl and nuke, covered, for 10 to 12 minutes. Remove from the micro-wave, let cool, and pour into a blender, pureeing until smooth. Return the mixture to a bowl, stir in the milk, and nuke until heated through.

"NO TIE NECESSARY" THAI TOMATO SOUP

You don't gotta get dressed up to have a fancy soup for dinner.

MAKES 4 SERVINGS

- 1 (15-ounce) can sweet corn (can substitute baby corn if preferred)
- 1 (13-ounce) can coconut milk
- 1 (10.7-ounce) can condensed tomato soup
- ¼ cup fresh cilantro, chopped (optional)
- Salt and pepper, to taste

Mix all the ingredients in a container. Heat, partially covered, for 2 minutes. Stir. Repeat this process until the soup is thoroughly heated and mixed.

CHEAPSKATE CHILI AND BEAN STEW

If you're strapped for cash, don't harvest your organs—buy kidney beans instead.

——————————— MAKES 4 SERVINGS ———————————

- 1 (15-ounce) can black beans, undrained
- 1 (15-ounce) can black-eyed peas, undrained
- 1 (15-ounce) can enchilada sauce (preferably green-chili style)
- 1 (15-ounce) can kidney beans, undrained
- 1 (14-ounce) can diced tomatoes, undrained
- ½ cup chickpeas, undrained
- Salt and pepper, to taste
- Corn or tortilla chips

Put all the ingredients in a bowl, except for the chips, and microwave on high for 4 minutes until hot. Serve with chips.

HAAS PARTY AVOCADO SOUP

Tired of the same old played-out house party? Print out some flyers and tell the gang the soup's on at your place this Saturday night. Okay, don't actually make flyers, but double the batch of soup if you're nice enough to share!

— MAKES 2 SERVINGS —

- 2 Haas avocados, cut in half with pits removed
- 2 cups original soy milk
- 1 tablespoon lime juice
- Salt and pepper, to taste

Scoop the avocado flesh into a bowl and mash it up. Mix in the milk and heat it in the microwave for 2 minutes. Take the bowl out and add the lime juice, salt, and pepper and heat for another 2 minutes. Eat.

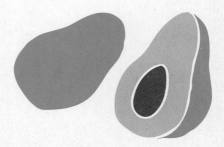

PJ PUMPKIN SOUP

Yup, you can pretend to be fancy while
staying in your pj's. Don't act like you ever
change out of your pj's anyway.

— MAKES 2 SERVINGS —

- 1 (15-ounce) can pumpkin puree
- 1 cup original soy milk
- 1 cup veggie broth
- 1 tablespoon olive oil
- Salt and pepper, to taste

Combine all the ingredients in a bowl and mix well. Nuke for 3 minutes or until hot. Stir again and serve!

SASSY-ASS
SOUTHWEST CHILI

This is a Mexi-Texi treat that'll sass your taste buds
like a Texas beauty queen in her terrible tweens.

—— MAKES 4 SERVINGS ——

- 1 (15-ounce) can vegan chili
- 1 (14.5-ounce) can fire-roasted diced tomatoes with green chiles
- 1 (8-ounce) can mushroom stems and pieces, drained
- ½ cup veggie burger crumbles
- Vegan cheddar cheese shreds, to taste
- Taco seasoning, to taste

Mix all the ingredients together and microwave 1 ½ to 2 minutes, until hot.

HALF-ASSED CHILI

When yummy chili is the goal but you don't want
to spend more than 5 minutes making it happen,
bust out this recipe. It's kind of like riding out
those final three credits with a pottery class.

—————— MAKES 4 SERVINGS ——————

- 1 (16-ounce) jar salsa
- 1 (15-ounce) can black beans, drained and rinsed
- 1 (15-ounce) can chili beans, undrained
- 1 (8.75-ounce) can corn kernels, drained
- ½ (4-ounce) can jalapeños

Combine everything in a bowl. Cover and nuke until hot, about 4
minutes, stirring occasionally.

PEACE RALLY PEA SOUP

C'mon, give peas a chance!

─────────── MAKES 2 SERVINGS ───────────

- 1 (12-ounce) package frozen peas
- ½ to 1 cup veggie broth
- Pinch each of sugar, salt, and pepper
- ¼ cup vegan sour cream

Cook the peas in the microwave, about 45 seconds to 1 minute, until tender but not overly wrinkly. Drain, place in a blender, and blend until souplike in texture, adding the veggie broth as necessary (you want a nice, thick soup, so don't add too much). Remove from the blender and put back into the dish you microwaved the peas in, adding the sugar, salt, and pepper. Heat for about 1 minute. Divide into bowls and swirl a little sour cream into each before serving!

SPOTLIGHT ON: RAMEN

RAMEN IS LIKELY ONE OF THOSE FOODS YOU'VE counted on more times than you can remember. When you're broke and hungry, ramen is there for you. Why not do something nice for ramen in return? Dress it up! You can do an endless number of things to deck out your ramen, so try all of our suggestions and then get creative and make up your own!

NOTE:
. . . .

Not all ramen noodles are vegan, so be sure to check the package!

───── DID YOU KNOW? ─────

Milk from cows is meant to be consumed by baby calves only—just like how we drink milk from our mothers as babies. We are the only species that drinks another species' breast milk and the only species that drinks breast milk past infancy. Weird, right?

ANCIENT JAPANESE NOODLE SECRET SALAD

The secret? It's cheap, easy, and damn good.

————— MAKES 2 SERVINGS —————

- ¼ cup sugar
- ¼ cup vegetable oil
- ¼ cup vinegar
- 1 teaspoon soy sauce
- 2 packages vegan ramen noodles (seasoning packets not needed)
- ½ pound shredded lettuce of your choice
- 1 (10-ounce) can mandarin orange segments, drained
- ¼ cup slivered almonds

In a bowl, mix together the sugar, oil, vinegar, and soy sauce to make the dressing. Nuke until the sugar dissolves, about 1 minute. Mix well and let cool. Crush the ramen noodles in the packages and pour them into the salad dressing. Dump the lettuce on a plate or in a bowl, sprinkle the oranges and almonds on top, and top with the dressing/ramen mixture. Enjoy!

RAMEN HOLIDAY

Ramen for those fancier occasions.

MAKES 1 SERVING

- 1 package vegan ramen
- 1 cup frozen mixed Italian veggies

Place the ramen noodles and veggies in a bowl. Add water according to the directions on the ramen package and nuke for 4 minutes or until the veggies are hot. Add the seasoning packet and eat. Yum!

"PIMP MY RAMEN" NOODLES

Spice up that raggedy package of ramen you've had since freshman year.

=== MAKES 1 SERVING ===

- 1 package vegan ramen (such as oriental flavor)
- 1 heaping tablespoon peanut butter
- 1 tablespoon sriracha

Crush the ramen and place in a large bowl. Cover with water and stir in the seasoning packet. Nuke for 4 minutes, remove from the microwave, drain the liquid, and add the peanut butter and sriracha, mixing well.

NOTE:

Best when served topped with fresh bean sprouts and crushed peanuts.

RENT'S DUE "CHEEZY" RAMEN

You gotta pay the man, but you gotta eat too. Stick it to him with this easy and filling bite you can totally afford after you search your roommate's pockets for change.

───── MAKES 1 SERVING ─────

- 1 package vegan ramen
- 2 tablespoons nutritional yeast

Cook the noodles according to the directions on the package and drain the excess water. Add the seasoning packet and nutritional yeast, and stir.

DORM-ROOM RAMEN DELIGHT

Tricked-out pasta for budding but broke foodies.

──────── MAKES 1 SERVING ────────

- 1 package vegan ramen noodles (seasoning packet not needed)
- 1 teaspoon vegan margarine
- Garlic powder, to taste
- Nutritional yeast, to taste
- Salt and pepper, to taste

Cook the ramen noodles in the microwave in just enough water to cover them. Drain. Add the margarine and sprinkle with the garlic powder, salt, pepper, and nutritional yeast. Stir together and eat.

FRESHASAURUS MEX RAMEN CASSEROLE

Everyone knows that ramen's been around
since dinosaurs ruled the Earth, so try this
fresh take on a Cretaceous Period classic.

—— MAKES 4 SERVINGS ——

- 6 cups water
- 3 packages vegan ramen noodles
  (seasoning packets not needed)
- 2 (15-ounce) cans vegan chili
- 1 (15-ounce) can tomatoes
- ½ to 1 cup shredded vegan cheddar cheese

Put water in a 3-quart casserole dish. Cover with a lid and nuke for 3 minutes. Remove from the microwave. Crush the ramen inside the packages and dump the noodles into the dish. Cover and nuke for 5 minutes, stirring halfway through. Remove and drain. Put the noodles back in the casserole dish, add the chili and the undrained tomatoes, and toss well. Cover and return to the microwave, nuking for 5 minutes or until hot throughout. Remove from the microwave, sprinkle with the cheese, replace the cover, and let stand until the cheese melts.

SAUCES AND DRESSINGS

THE FRENCH HAVE SOME PRETTY GREAT IDEAS—YOU know, like the bicycle, the sewing machine, and, more importantly, the French kiss—so you should listen to 'em when they say sauces and dressings can absolutely make or break a dish. Think about it: if you have the most amazing, melt-in-your-mouth mashed potatoes and then pile some nasty-tasting gravy on top, your taters are ruined, right? We promise that our sauces and dressings will keep your dishes oh so lovely, or you can come to our office and we'll grovel at your feet and beg for your forgiveness. Okay, so maybe not. But we will pat you on the back and say, "Better luck next time, champ."

DID YOU KNOW?

It takes more than 2,400 gallons of water to produce just 1 pound of meat. Only 25 gallons of water are required to grow 1 pound of wheat. You can save more water by not eating a pound of meat than you can by not showering for six months!

SUPER-CHEEZY SAUCE

Carbalicious over rice or pasta, this sauce
is cheesier than your roommate's corkboard
collage of her high school friends.

———— MAKES 2 SERVINGS ————

- ⅓ cup nutritional yeast
- 1 tablespoon soy sauce
- 1 tablespoon olive oil
- 2 tablespoons water, plus more to desired consistency
- Pepper, to taste

Blend all the ingredients together until smooth, adding more water if needed. Pop in the microwave for 1 minute or until warm. Add liberally to cooked rice, pasta, or broccoli.

RAUNCHY DRESSING

Your roomie's sock is on the doorknob again, so you might as well order a vegan pizza and make some ranch dressing to dip it in—it might be a while.

MAKES 8 SERVINGS

- 1 cup vegan mayonnaise
- ¼ cup original soy milk
- 2 overflowing teaspoons dried parsley
- 1 ½ teaspoons apple cider vinegar
- ½ teaspoon black pepper
- ½ teaspoon garlic powder
- ½ teaspoon onion powder
- ½ teaspoon salt
- ¼ teaspoon dried dill

Put all the ingredients in a bowl and mix until creamy. For even tastier results, refrigerate before using.

BADASS BALSAMIC VINAIGRETTE

Break out the iceberg and eat like a boss.

—————————— MAKES 2 SERVINGS ——————————

- 2 tablespoons balsamic vinegar
- 2 tablespoons seasoned rice vinegar
- 2 tablespoons water
- 2 teaspoons garlic powder
- Olive oil, to taste

Mix all the ingredients together in a small bowl. Use on salads or to dip bread in.

"DRESS TO IMPRESS" CITRUS DRESSING

Drizzling this light and flavorful dressing over an ordinary salad is kinda the opposite of wearing your pj's to class. It's good to get dressed up now and then.

MAKES 8 SERVINGS

- 1 cup olive oil
- ¾ cup orange juice
- 6 tablespoons mustard
- Salt and pepper, to taste

Put all the ingredients in a blender and blend until smooth. Serve over mixed greens or the salad of your choice.

SWEETIE'S NO-HONEY MUSTARD

Because real honey mustard is a total buzzkill.

MAKES 1 SERVING

- 2 tablespoons Dijon mustard
- 1 tablespoon sugar
- ½ teaspoon rice vinegar

Combine all three ingredients in a small container and mix well. Good on salad or for dipping vegan chicken tenders!

AWESOME ASIAN SAUCE

The word "awesome" is in the name—
do you really need to know more?

MAKES 1 SERVING

- 2 tablespoons brown sugar
- 1 tablespoon rice vinegar
- ½ tablespoon soy sauce
- ¼ teaspoon garlic powder
- Pepper, to taste

Combine all ingredients and mix well. Serve over veggies and tofu. Also a great dipping sauce for spring rolls.

BEST-O PESTO SAUCE

Warning: this sauce is highly addictive
when combined with...everything.

————— MAKES 4 SERVINGS —————

- 2 cups packed fresh basil leaves
- ½ cup pine nuts
- ¼ cup hot water
- ¼ cup olive oil
- ¼ teaspoon garlic powder
- Salt, to taste

Combine all ingredients in a blender and blend until smooth.
Serve over pasta or dip your pizza into it!

THOUSAND-TIMES-BETTER SALAD DRESSING

Because when else are you allowed to put mayo and ketchup on a salad?!

MAKES 8 SERVINGS

- 1 cup vegan mayonnaise
- ⅓ cup ketchup
- 3 tablespoons sweet pickle relish
- ½ teaspoon onion powder
- ¼ teaspoon salt
- ⅛ teaspoon garlic powder

Stir all the ingredients together in a bowl.

ENDLESS SRIRACHA MAYO

OK, so clearly this sauce isn't actually endless, but you'll wish it was. Hurry and make more!

MAKES 4 SERVINGS

- ½ cup vegan mayonnaise
- 2 tablespoons sriracha, or to taste

Stir the mayo and sriracha together until the mixture is a nice pinkish color. Dip your fries or vegan chicken tenders into it, or use it as a burger spread!

VEGAN BLUE CHEESE

*Is it a dip? Is it a dressing? It's hard to know
for sure, but we do know it's delicious.*

MAKES 8 SERVINGS

- 1 cup vegan mayonnaise
- ½ teaspoon garlic powder
- Lemon juice, to taste (start with a few squirts)
- ¼ teaspoon apple cider vinegar
- ¼ (14-ounce) block of firm tofu, drained
- Salt and pepper, to taste
- Dried parsley, to taste

Mix the mayo, garlic powder, lemon juice, and apple cider vinegar until well combined. Crumble the tofu into the mayo mixture, add salt, pepper, and parsley, then stir to combine.

DINNER

WARNING: ONCE YOU START MAKING THESE DINNER delights, the delicious aroma will waft down the hall and you'll need to fight off the moochers with a stick…or at least charge admission at the door. These dishes will fill you up and fool all of your friends into thinking you're a culinary genius.

DID YOU KNOW?

Many of history's greatest minds were vegetarian, such as: Pythagoras, Socrates, Plato, Clement of Alexandria, Plutarch, King Ashoka, Leonardo da Vinci, Michel de Montaigne, Akbar, John Milton, Sir Isaac Newton, Emanuel Swedenborg, Voltaire, Benjamin Franklin, Jean-Jacques Rousseau, Alphonse de Lamartine, Percy Bysshe Shelley, Ralph Waldo Emerson, Henry David Thoreau, Leo Tolstoy, George Bernard Shaw, Rabindranath Tagore, Mahatma Gandhi, Albert Schweitzer, Rosa Parks, Alice Walker, Angela Davis, Coretta Scott King, Pattrice Jones, and Albert Einstein.

SILENCE OF THE LAMBS SHEPHERD'S PIE

Why are the lambs quiet? 'Cuz they're not being turned into meat pies! "Beefy" enough to fool even the most cultured cannibals, so get the Chianti out and invite all of your Little Bo Peeps over for dinner.

MAKES 4 SERVINGS

- 2 servings instant vegan potatoes
- 1 (12-ounce) package veggie burger crumbles
- 1 (14.5-ounce) can mixed veggies (peas and carrots), drained
- 1 (8.75-ounce) can of corn, drained
- 3 tablespoons veggie broth
- Salt and pepper, to taste

Cook the instant mashed potatoes according to the package directions. Set aside. Microwave the veggie burger crumbles for 1 ½ minutes. Mix the crumbles with the veggies and veggie broth in a bowl. Top with mashed potatoes, sprinkle on salt and pepper, and nuke for another minute or until hot.

CUTE-CUMBER SUSHI BOWL

You + cute classmate + matchstick cukes
= match made in math class.

=== MAKES 1 SERVING ===

- 1 (10-ounce) bag microwavable frozen white rice
- 1 tablespoon rice vinegar
- 1 teaspoon sugar
- Pinch of salt
- ½ avocado, peeled, pitted, and chopped
- ½ cucumber, sliced like thick matchsticks
- 1 sheet roasted nori seaweed, torn into small pieces
- Soy sauce, to taste
- Wasabi and pickled ginger (optional)

Cook the rice according to the package directions. Mix the rice, vinegar, sugar, and salt in a medium-size bowl. Top off with avocado, cucumber, and nori—arrange it nicely if you're feelin' fancy. Serve with the soy sauce and add wasabi and ginger.

WTF? WINGS

Amaze your meat-eating friends with this "tastes-like-the-real-thing" alternative. So scrumptious, you'll have them dragging themselves to the nearest market to get their own fixin's.

MAKES 2 SERVINGS

- 2 (8-ounce) bags vegan chicken strips
- ⅓ cup soy sauce
- 1 cup fine cracker crumbs
- ½ teaspoon garlic powder
- ⅛ teaspoon pepper

Thaw the chicken strips. Pour the soy sauce into a bowl and set aside. In another bowl, combine the cracker crumbs, garlic powder, and pepper. Dip the chicken in the soy sauce, and roll in the seasoned crumbs, coating evenly. Arrange on a plate and cover with paper towels. Microwave on high for 5 minutes or until hot. Serve with your favorite dipping sauce from the last chapter.

F-U TACOS

These tacos put the "fu" in tofu.

—————— MAKES 4 SERVINGS ——————

- 1 (12-ounce) package silken firm tofu
- 1 (1-ounce) packet vegan taco seasoning
- 1 (16-ounce) can vegetarian refried beans
- 4 taco shells
- Shredded lettuce, vegan cheese, tomato, etc. (optional)

Put the tofu and seasoning mix in a blender and blend until smooth. Transfer to a medium-size bowl. Fold in the beans. Nuke for 2 to 3 minutes or until hot, stirring halfway through. Fill the taco shells with the tofu mixture and top with your favorite taco toppers.

NO-BEEF STROGANOFF

So easy you can make this blindfolded, but don't hold it against us if you spill tomato sauce all over your roommate's term paper.

MAKES 4 SERVINGS

- ½ (16-ounce) package vegan pasta of choice
- 1 (12-ounce) package veggie burger crumbles
- 1 cup sliced fresh mushrooms
- ¼ cup tomato sauce
- 2 teaspoons onion powder
- 1 teaspoon mustard
- ½ teaspoon sugar
- ¼ teaspoon salt
- Pepper, to taste
- 1 cup vegan sour cream
- ¼ to ½ cup soy milk

Submerge the noodles in water in a bowl and nuke for 5 minutes. Stir and repeat until thoroughly cooked. Drain completely. Empty the crumbles into a large, microwave-safe bowl and nuke for about 2 minutes, stirring halfway through. They won't be heated all the way, but that's fine. Add the next seven ingredients to the bowl and nuke for 3 minutes or until hot, stirring halfway through. Mix in the sour cream and soy milk right before serving. Serve over noodles.

NO-GRIEF "BEEF" NOODLES

We promise, neither you nor any cow will be harmed in the making of these easy, "cheesy," nuked noodles.

MAKES 4 SERVINGS

- 6 ounces noodles
- 1 (12-ounce) package veggie burger crumbles, thawed
- 1 cup shredded vegan mozzarella cheese
- 2 tablespoons vegan mayonnaise
- 1 tablespoon water
- Salt and pepper, to taste

Submerge the noodles in water in a bowl and nuke for 5 minutes. Stir and repeat until thoroughly cooked. Drain completely. Put the veggie burger crumbles, cheese, mayonnaise, water, salt, and pepper in a large bowl and stir together. Nuke for 1 minute. Stir, add the noodles, and nuke for 1 more minute or until hot.

WHITE BEAN "ALFREDO" CANOODLES

A classy dish to share with that classy coed
you were seen canoodling with in the quad.

—— MAKES 2 TO 3 SERVINGS ——

- ½ (14-ounce) package vegan pasta of choice
- 1 to 2 tablespoons vegan margarine
- 1 (15-ounce) can white beans, rinsed and drained
- ¾ to 1 cup unsweetened original soy or almond milk
- ¼ teaspoon garlic powder
- ¼ teaspoon onion powder
- ¼ teaspoon salt, plus more to taste
- Pepper, to taste

Submerge the noodles in water in a bowl and nuke for 5 minutes. Stir and repeat until thoroughly cooked. Drain completely. While the pasta is cooking through, place the margarine in a mug and nuke for 20 to 25 seconds, until melted. Pour the margarine into a blender along with the white beans, ¾ cup of milk, garlic powder, onion powder, and salt. Blend until completely smooth. If the sauce is too thick, add the remaining milk until the sauce reaches the desired consistency. Pour the sauce into a microwave-safe bowl, then season with pepper and more salt as needed. Nuke for about 1 minute, until heated through. Serve over pasta!

LEGUME VA-VA-VOOM

The ultimate impress-a-date dish, we guarantee
that dinner will go over really well. However,
we can in no way promise that you won't be
dealt the friend card during dessert.

MAKES 6 SERVINGS

- 2 (10-ounce) bags frozen brown rice
- 1 to 2 large, ripe avocados
- ½ (15-ounce) can lentils
- ½ cup chopped peanuts
- Salt and pepper, to taste
- 6 large romaine lettuce leaves

Cook the rice according to the package directions. Before the rice cools completely, halve the avocados, remove the pits, scoop out the pulp, and mash it into the rice. When the ingredients have blended, add the lentils and peanuts. Season with salt and pepper. Serve portions on top of the romaine leaves. Bon appétit!

MICRO-RITOS

All you need is a microwave for an instant fiesta. Okay,
some amigos and a bottle of tequila would be nice too,
but don't blame us if you get busted by the RA.

MAKES 4 SERVINGS

- 1 (9-ounce) bag vegan chicken strips
- 1 (16-ounce) jar salsa
- 1 (15-ounce) can black or pinto beans, drained
- 1 cup shredded Mexican-style vegan cheese
- 1 (10-ounce) bag frozen rice, brown or white
- 4 (10-inch) flour tortillas
- 1 avocado, peeled, pitted, and sliced (optional)

Nuke the chicken in a large, microwave-safe bowl for about 2 minutes or until cooked through. Add the salsa (reserving a small bit to top off the burritos), beans, and cheese to the chicken, and nuke for about 2 minutes or until hot. Nuke the frozen rice according to the package directions. Pour the rice into the chicken mixture and mix well. Nuke the tortillas between two damp paper towels for a few seconds to warm and soften. Spoon the mixture into the tortillas, top with the rest of the salsa and avocado, roll up, and eat.

"TASTES LIKE CHICKEN" STRIPS

Meaty enough to fool hardcore carnivores, but we promise—they're as fake as your ID.

MAKES 4 SERVINGS

- ¾ cup vegan mayonnaise
- ½ cup Italian salad dressing
- 2 tablespoons vinegar
- 2 tablespoons water
- 2 (8-ounce) bags vegan chicken strips

Mix everything but the chicken in a bowl. Pour the mixture into a large Ziploc bag, add the chicken, and let it marinate for 30 minutes (flip the bag every five minutes to evenly marinate). Pour the mixture onto a large plate and nuke for 2 minutes. These are great on their own or served with rice.

NOT YOUR AVERAGE BURRITO

Stuffed with vegan chicken, brown rice, and broccoli,
this burrito is weirder than that kid in the single
room down the hall with garlic cloves hanging
from the ceiling. But it's delicious, trust us!

MAKES 1 SERVING

- 5 vegan chicken strips
- ⅓ cup frozen broccoli florets
- ¼ cup microwavable brown rice
- 1 (10-inch) tortilla
- ¼ to ⅓ cup shredded vegan cheddar cheese
- Salsa, to taste

Cook the chicken, broccoli, and brown rice in the microwave according to each package's instructions. Set aside. Warm the tortillas in the microwave for 10 seconds. Top each tortilla with the rice, broccoli, chicken, cheese, and salsa; roll into a burrito; and enjoy!

LEAVE-OUT-THE-NOODLES LASAGNA

No noodles? No problem! Stuff your stomach with this super-easy lasagna and get your Italian fix.

=== MAKES 4 SERVINGS ===

- 1 (14-ounce) package firm tofu, drained and mashed
- 1 tablespoon lemon juice
- 2 teaspoons dried basil
- ¾ teaspoon salt
- ½ teaspoon garlic powder
- 1 (12-ounce) package vegan sausage, crumbled
- 1 (28-ounce) jar marinara sauce
- 1 or 2 (16-ounce) cans of artichoke hearts, drained and chopped
- 1 (10-ounce) bag frozen peas, thawed
- 2 tablespoons olive oil

Mix the tofu, lemon juice, basil, salt, and garlic powder together in a large bowl. Set aside. Nuke sausage in the microwave for 2 minutes or until warm. Cover the bottom of a large bowl with marinara sauce. Toss in all the ingredients and top with the remaining marinara sauce. Nuke for 5 minutes or until hot.

CHICK MAGNET "CHICKEN" CASSEROLE

Chicks totally dig a guy who cooks for them. This easy-to-make and downright impressive-looking dish is a sure thing, so how about laying off the cheap cologne there, Ace?

MAKES 6 SERVINGS

- 2 (8-ounce) bags frozen vegan chicken strips
- 1 (14-ounce) package firm tofu, drained and mashed
- 2 stalks celery, sliced very thin
- ¼ cup nutritional yeast
- 1 teaspoon garlic powder
- 1 teaspoon salt
- ½ teaspoon pepper
- 1 (15-ounce) can diced tomatoes with green chiles
- ½ (10-ounce) bag tortilla chips
- 1 (8-ounce) bag vegan cheddar cheese shreds

Thaw the chicken strips and chop into bite-size pieces, then set aside. Combine the tofu, celery, nutritional yeast, garlic powder, salt, and pepper in a medium-size bowl, stirring until the mixture is well blended. Add the tomatoes and stir. Set aside. Cover the bottom of a lightly greased 2-quart casserole dish with tortilla chips, half of the chicken, half of the tomato/tofu mixture, and a third of the cheese. Repeat the layers, then top with the remaining tortilla chips and cheese. Cover the dish with waxed paper or a lid and nuke for 7 minutes. Uncover and nuke for 4 more minutes or until heated thoroughly.

THE BURNING BIBIMBAP BOWL

This is a Korean-inspired meal in a bowl guaranteed to bring on the burn. A good burn though—not the kind that sends you to the health center.

MAKES 2 SERVINGS

- 1 (10-ounce) bag frozen rice
- 2 teaspoons hot pepper paste
- 2 teaspoons sesame tahini
- 2 teaspoons soy sauce
- 2 teaspoons vegetable oil

Cook the rice according to the package directions and set aside. Combine the remaining ingredients in a small bowl. Split the cooked rice between two bowls, then add half of the mixture to each bowl of rice and mix well. Enjoy!

PANTRY RAID PASTA

Nothing to eat? Don't get your granny panties in a bunch. There are always noodles hiding in your cupboard. If not, run down the hall, burst into your neighbors' rooms, and raid their pantries.

—— MAKES 6 SERVINGS ——

- 1 (16-ounce) box elbow pasta
- 1 (15-ounce) can diced tomatoes
- 2 (8-ounce) bags vegan chicken strips
- Salt and pepper, to taste

Put the pasta in a large bowl and fill the bowl with water until the pasta is submerged (you may need to split the pasta in half and do one half at a time). Cook on high for 5 minutes, stir, and repeat until tender. Drain the excess water. Set the drained pasta aside. Cook the chicken strips for 2 minutes or until heated through. Pour the pasta on a plate and top with the diced tomatoes, chicken, salt, and pepper. Heat for 1 more minute, and voila!

AFTER DELIVERY HOURS STIR-FRY

Delivery hours are over and you're hungry.
Make your own stir-fry (no wok required)!

MAKES 4 SERVINGS

- 2 servings microwavable rice
- 1 (16-ounce) bag frozen mixed vegetables
- 1 (14-ounce) can baby corn
- 1 (8-ounce) can bamboo shoots
- 1 (8-ounce) can water chestnuts
- Soy sauce, to taste

Cook the rice according to the package directions and set aside. Dump the bag of veggies in a bowl and nuke for 4 minutes or until warm. Add the corn, bamboo shoots, and water chestnuts, and nuke for an additional 2 minutes. Add soy sauce and place veggies on top of rice.

ROAD TRIP RED BEANS AND RICE

Fill up with a hot and spicy punch of
protein before you hit the road.

— MAKES 2 SERVINGS —

- 1 (10-ounce) bag frozen rice
- 1 (16-ounce) can dark red kidney beans, drained
- 1 (14.5-ounce) can diced tomatoes, drained
- 1 (4-ounce) can mild green chiles
- Hot sauce, to taste

Cook the rice in the microwave according to the package directions. Combine all the ingredients in a large bowl and heat for 3 minutes or until hot.

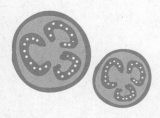

BETTER THAN THE "BELL" BURRITO

Yeah, you could just go to the drive-thru burrito joint, but why bother when you can make it at home?

━━ MAKES 3 SERVINGS ━━

- ½ cup salsa
- ½ cup vegan cream cheese
- 1 tablespoon hot sauce
- Salt, to taste
- ½ tablespoon lime juice
- 1 avocado, peeled, pitted, and mashed
- 3 (8-inch) flour tortillas
- 2 cups fresh baby spinach
- ½ cup canned corn
- 1 (2.25-ounce) can sliced black olives

Combine the salsa, cream cheese, hot sauce, and salt in a small bowl. Pour the lime juice over the mashed avocado in another small bowl. Spread about 2 tablespoons of the cream cheese mixture on each tortilla, place 2 rows of spinach leaves in the center of each tortilla, then top each row with avocado, corn, and black olives. Roll the tortillas up tightly. For a wet burrito, top with more salsa.

BROCKIN' RICE PILAF

Tastes like something from a swanky restaurant, without any of the fuss. Feel free to wipe your mouth on your sleeve.

―――――――― MAKES 4 SERVINGS ――――――――

- 1 cup microwavable rice
- 3 cups veggie broth
- 1 (10-ounce) bag frozen chopped broccoli
- Salt and pepper, to taste

Cook the microwavable rice in the veggie broth, instead of water, following all other directions on the package. Take out and set aside. Cook the broccoli in the microwave for 4 minutes or until heated. Mix the broccoli and rice together and add salt and pepper as needed.

GUAC WRAPS

A Mexican take on a lettuce wrap. Wash it down
with a glass of horchata (cinnamon rice milk),
close your eyes, and pretend you're in Mexico.

MAKES 1 SERVING

- ½ cup corn kernels
- ¼ cup guacamole (store-bought or
  use the recipe on page 211)
- ¼ cup salsa
- 1 tablespoon lime juice
- ½ teaspoon garlic powder
- ½ teaspoon onion powder
- 2 large lettuce leaves

Mix everything but the lettuce leaves together in a bowl. Divide
in half and plop in the middle of the two lettuce leaves. Roll them
up into burritos and eat.

PEAS 'N' RICE IS NICE

When you're short on time and dinner ideas, peas and rice is always nice. It's quick, cheap, and filling, so try not to doze off when you're done—you were in a hurry, remember?

MAKES 2 SERVINGS

- 1 (10-ounce) bag frozen rice
- ½ (14.5-ounce) can peas
- 2 tablespoons canned diced tomatoes, drained
- Garlic powder, to taste
- Salt, to taste

Cook the rice according to the package directions and set aside. Put the peas and tomatoes in a bowl and nuke for about 1 ½ minutes or until hot. Add the peas and tomatoes to the cooked rice and sprinkle on some garlic powder and salt. Mix together and eat.

RICHIE RICE

You can eat like royalty and still manage
to pay off your student loans.

MAKES 2 SERVINGS

- 2 cups microwavable rice
- 1 (14.5-ounce) can vegan butternut squash soup
- ½ cup vegan parmesan cheese
- Garlic powder, to taste
- Onion powder, to taste
- Salt, to taste

Cook the rice according to the package directions. Put everything in a large bowl, stir well, and nuke for about 1 ½ minutes or until hot. Stir before serving.

TEXAS RANGER ROLL UPS

Chuck Norris doesn't eat these Tex-Mex roll ups. He forces them into submission.

—————————— MAKES 4 SERVINGS ——————————

- 1 (15.5-ounce) can corn, drained
- 1 (15-ounce) can black beans, rinsed and drained
- 2 tablespoons lime juice
- 2 tablespoons orange juice
- 2 teaspoons chopped chives
- 2 teaspoons garlic powder
- ⅛ teaspoon salt
- 4 flour or corn tortillas
- Salsa, to taste

Mix all the ingredients together except the tortillas and the salsa. Spoon the mixture onto the tortillas, roll them up tightly, and top with salsa.

ALL-NIGHTER NACHOS

Bad news: your ten-page paper is due at 8:00
a.m. tomorrow and you haven't started it yet.
Good news: noshing on these zesty, protein-
packed nachos will nix your chances of nodding
off before you finish the footnotes.

—— MAKES 4 SERVINGS ——

- 1 (12-ounce) package veggie burger crumbles
- 1 (16-ounce) jar chunky salsa
- 1 (1-ounce) packet taco seasoning
- 2 teaspoons onion powder
- 1 bag of your favorite tortilla chips

Nuke the crumbles in a large bowl until warm, about 1 minute.
Stir in the remaining ingredients and serve on top of tortilla chips.

GIZMO'S GLAZED CHICK'N

Hungry like a gremlin after midnight? Squash those mad Mogwai munchies with this sweet and tangy rice dish.

MAKES 2 SERVINGS

- 2 tablespoons Italian dressing
- 1 tablespoon apricot preserves
- 1 (8-ounce) bag vegan chicken strips, thawed

Mix together the dressing and the preserves in a bowl. Put in a large resealable bag with the chicken and shake. Let sit in fridge for 30 minutes. Put on a plate and nuke for 30 seconds. Great alone or served with rice.

BY THE TEXTBOOK TEMPEH TACOS

A textbook example of why tempeh should be
used often and in large, delicious quantities.

- 1 (8-ounce) package tempeh
- 1 tablespoon water
- ⅓ (1-ounce) packet taco seasoning
- ¼ cup salsa, plus more to taste
- 2 to 3 (10-inch) tortillas
- ½ cup guacamole
- Fixings of choice

Crumble the tempeh in a bowl and nuke for 2 minutes or until hot. Add the water and taco seasoning. Stir it up and add as much salsa as you'd like. Scoop into the tortillas, top with guacamole and other fixings according to your taste (like lettuce, tomatoes, etc.), and have a Tex-Mex kind of night.

CURE-ALL NOODLES

Move over, chicken soup. These creamy, comforting noodles have been proven to heal a variety of ailments, including but not limited to failed tests, homesickness, hangovers, and cafeteria food–induced starvation.

MAKES 4 SERVINGS

- 1 (16-ounce) package pasta of your choice
- ½ (28-ounce) jar marinara sauce
- ½ (12-ounce) container vegan sour cream
- ½ (8-ounce) container vegan cream cheese

Cook the noodles by submerging them in water in a microwave-safe dish and nuking for about 5 minutes. Stir and repeat until completely cooked. Drain and set aside. Mix together the remaining ingredients in a separate bowl and nuke for 1 minute. Place the noodles on a plate and top with the sauce.

MAKE A REAL MEAL "MEATY" SPAGHETTI

Can you survive on Twizzlers, Fruit Loops, and
Red Bull? Uh, yeah. Should you? Hell no!

MAKES 4 SERVINGS

- 1 (16-ounce) package spaghetti
- 1 (14-ounce) tube vegan sausage
- 2 tablespoons olive oil
- 1 tablespoon garlic powder
- Italian herbs, to taste
- Salt and pepper, to taste
- 1 (28-ounce) jar marinara sauce

Break the spaghetti in half, place in a bowl, and submerge in water. Nuke for 5 minutes, stir, and repeat until thoroughly cooked. Remove from the microwave, drain, and set aside. Break the sausage into bite-size pieces. Place in another bowl along with the olive oil, garlic powder, Italian herbs, salt, and pepper. Nuke for approximately 5 minutes or until the sausage is sizzling. Pour in the jar of sauce. Cover loosely with plastic wrap and nuke for 1 to 2 minutes or until hot, stirring halfway through. Toss the spaghetti with the sauce and serve.

AFTER-PARTY AGLIO E OLIO

Impress that hottie you brought back to your room after a long night out by making (and correctly pronouncing) this steamy Italian snack. Need a hint, Romeo? It's ah-leo e oh-leo.

—— MAKES 2 SERVINGS ——

- ½ (16-ounce) box spaghetti
- 1 (14.5-ounce) can diced tomatoes, drained
- 1 tablespoon olive oil
- 1 teaspoon garlic powder
- ½ teaspoon salt
- 1 tablespoon vegan margarine

Submerge the noodles in water and cook in the microwave for 5 minutes, stir, and repeat until tender. Meanwhile, mix the tomatoes, oil, garlic powder, and salt. Take the spaghetti out of the microwave, drain, and toss onto a plate. Add the margarine to the oil mixture and microwave until the margarine is melted. Pour over the spaghetti and toss.

BBCUTIE CHICKPEAS

Saucier than a pissed-off Southern sorority girl, y'all.

MAKES 2 SERVINGS

- 1 (15-ounce) can chickpeas, drained
- ½ cup BBQ sauce
- ¼ teaspoon onion powder

Mix chickpeas, BBQ sauce, and onion powder together in a big bowl. Nuke on high for 2 minutes. Stir. Serve over rice.

NIGHT OWL NACHOS

Up till dawn cramming for a test? These "cheesy" nachos are the perfect culinary companion for any all-nighter.

──── MAKES 3 SERVINGS ────

- 1 (15-ounce) can black beans, drained
- 1 cup salsa
- ¼ cup nutritional yeast
- 1 bag tortilla chips
- 1 (10-ounce) can diced tomatoes, drained
- 1 teaspoon dried chives
- ¼ cup lettuce
- 3 tablespoons vegan sour cream
- Salt and pepper, to taste

Place the black beans in a bowl and heat in the microwave for 2 minutes. In another, smaller container, mix the salsa and the nutritional yeast together and heat for 1 minute. Arrange the chips on a plate and top with the beans, salsa-yeast mixture, diced tomatoes, chives, lettuce, and sour cream. Sprinkle with salt and pepper.

EXAM WEEK FUEL

Yes, it is perfectly possible to survive on quesadillas for an entire week. Just be sure to supplement with plenty of soda, coffee, and spontaneous, sleep deprivation— induced dorm room dance parties for a balanced diet.

MAKES 1 SERVING

- 2 (6-inch) flour tortillas
- ¼ cup shredded vegan cheddar cheese
- ¼ cup shredded vegan mozzarella cheese
- 2 vegan turkey deli slices
- 1 tablespoon pizza sauce

Place one of the tortillas on a plate. Spoon 2 tablespoons each of the cheddar and mozzarella cheeses over the tortilla. Cover with the turkey slices. Spread the sauce over the turkey and top with the remaining cheeses. Place the second tortilla on top. Cook in microwave until the cheese melts, about 1 ½ minutes. Allow to cool before cutting into wedges.

DROPOUT SPAGHETTI

You don't even have to boil water for this, which
automatically makes it easier than your chem lab.

――――――― MAKES 1 SERVING ―――――――

- 4 ounces pasta
- ¾ cup favorite marinara sauce
- ¾ cup veggie burger crumbles, thawed completely

Submerge the pasta in water in a large bowl and nuke for 5
minutes. Stir and repeat until thoroughly cooked. Remove from
the microwave and drain. Put back in the bowl, add the sauce and
the crumbles, and nuke for 1 minute.

SUPER-FRAGA-DELICIOUS TOSTADA PIZZA

Guaranteed to make you singing-and-dancing-with-cartoon-characters kind of happy.

—————— MAKES 3 SERVINGS ——————

- 1 cup vegetarian refried beans
- 6 tostada shells
- 3 to 4 tablespoons vegan enchilada sauce
- ½ cup shredded vegan cheddar cheese
- 2 stalks green onion, chopped
- 1 small tomato, chopped

Spread ¼ cup of the refried beans onto one tostada shell. Cover with another tostada. Spoon approximately 1 tablespoon enchilada sauce on top of the second tostada, sprinkle with a handful of cheese, then put the pizza into a microwave or toaster oven, and heat until the cheese is melted. Top with the green onions and tomatoes. Repeat with the other tostada shells.

"CHEAT MEAT" LOVERS BBQ PIZZA

It's okay to cheat. Well—at least in this case. Loaded with tons of vegan meat and smothered in mouthwatering BBQ sauce, cheating never tasted so good!

MAKES 4 SERVINGS

- 1 (8-ounce) bag vegan chicken strips
- ½ (12-ounce) package veggie burger crumbles
- ½ (12-ounce) package vegan sausage crumbles
- BBQ sauce, to taste
- A cheese-less pizza with your favorite veggies

Place all the meats in a bowl and nuke until defrosted, about 30 seconds. Remove from the microwave and cut up the chicken. Add the BBQ sauce to the bowl and stir. Nuke for 2 minutes or until hot. Dump onto the prepared pizza and chow down.

NOTE:

If you're lucky enough to have vegan cheese at your local pizzeria (tons of pizzerias offer vegan cheese these days—hit us up at peta2@peta2.com for more info) or frozen pizzas at a nearby grocery made with nondairy cheese, you should definitely get one of those to go with all this vegan meat!

MARIE'S CURRY

This red lentil curry has all of the elements you'll need to spark some chemistry with your hot lab partner.

MAKES 1 SERVING

- 1 ½ cups water
- ½ cup dried split red lentils
- ½ teaspoon curry powder
- ⅛ teaspoon garlic powder
- Salt and pepper, to taste

Put the water and lentils in a microwave-safe bowl and cook in the microwave, uncovered, for 12 to 13 minutes. Carefully remove from the microwave (use hot pads if you have 'em or a few T-shirts to pad your hands if you don't have any). Add the curry powder, garlic powder, salt, and pepper, then stir to combine. Delicious over rice or even eaten alone!

NOTE:

Keep any extra lentils you have on hand in a jar. It looks pretty, and every time you see the jar of lentils, you'll remember how ridiculously easy this recipe is and make it again!

BIG MAN ON CAMPUS BURRITO

Busting with beans and brown rice, this is the Bigfoot of burritos. It'll make you say fee-fi-fo-yum. (It's giant; get the picture?)

MAKES 4 SERVINGS

- 1 (10-ounce) bag frozen brown rice
- 1 (15-ounce) can black beans, drained
- 4 (10-inch) flour tortillas
- 1 cup shredded lettuce
- 1 (10-ounce) can diced tomatoes, drained
- ¼ cup salsa

Cook the rice according to the directions on the package, then set aside. Cook the beans for 30 seconds and set aside. Heat up the tortillas for 10 seconds each or until soft. Top the tortillas with the rice, beans, lettuce, and tomatoes, then roll up and top with salsa.

VEGAN MAC 'N' CHEEZ

Way better than that orange, powdery stuff.

——— MAKES 4 SERVINGS ———

- ½ (16-ounce) package elbow macaroni
- ½ cup original soy milk
- 5 tablespoons nutritional yeast
- ½ cup vegan margarine
- Salt, pepper, and garlic powder, to taste

Submerge the macaroni in water and nuke for 5 minutes; stir and repeat until completely cooked. Drain and set aside. Mix the soy milk and nutritional yeast together in the same bowl you used for the macaroni. Add the macaroni back in, along with the margarine. Mix well. If too thick, add a splash more of soy milk; if too thin, add another tablespoon of nutritional yeast. Add the salt, pepper, and garlic powder.

DIRTY RICE DONE DIRT CHEAP

Rice so cheap and dirty, it makes Uncle Ben blush.

—— MAKES 4 SERVINGS ——

- ¾ cup rice
- 1 ½ (14.5-ounce) cans whole peeled tomatoes, drained
- 1 cup tomato juice
- 1 cup veggie burger crumbles, thawed
- 1 (4-ounce) can diced green chiles
- 1 teaspoon onion powder
- ½ teaspoon salt

Cook the rice according to the directions on the package, then set aside. Combine the remaining ingredients in a bowl. Heat in the microwave for 2 minutes or until warm. Take out and mix in the rice. Eat.

HOT TOT CASSEROLE

You can "borrow" tater tots and green beans
from the caf if you need to, the same way
you "borrowed" all that silverware.

MAKES 4 SERVINGS

- 1 (32-ounce) package frozen tater tots
- 1 (10-ounce) block vegan cheddar cheese, shredded
- 1 ½ cups veggie broth
- 2 tablespoons vegan sour cream
- 1 (15-ounce) can green beans, drained
- 8 slices vegan ham, torn apart
- Salt and pepper, to taste

Put the tots in a large dish and nuke for 2 minutes or until no longer frozen. Place the shredded cheese in another bowl and nuke until it gets slightly melty. Add the broth and sour cream to the melty cheese and stir until well mixed; then mix in the green beans and ham. Add the tots and stir until everything is mixed together. Take a serving from the bowl, put it on a plate, and microwave for about 3 minutes or until hot. Repeat with remaining servings and eat.

FETTUCCINE ALESSANDRO

Alfredo's hotter vegan brother.

MAKES 4 SERVINGS

- 1 cup frozen cauliflower florets
- ½ (16-ounce) package fettuccine
- 1 cup original almond milk
- 2 tablespoons nutritional yeast
- ½ tablespoon lemon juice
- 1 teaspoon olive oil
- ½ teaspoon salt, plus more to taste
- ⅛ teaspoon garlic powder
- Pepper, to taste

Cook the cauliflower according to the package directions and set aside. Break the fettuccine in half, submerge in water in microwave-safe bowl, and heat in the microwave for 5 minutes. Stir and continue to microwave until tender. Drain the water and put the pasta back in the bowl. Put the cauliflower, almond milk, nutritional yeast, lemon juice, olive oil, salt, and garlic powder into the blender and blend until creamy and smooth. Taste and adjust spices if needed. Pour the sauce over the pasta, mix well, and heat in the microwave for another minute or until warm. Sprinkle with pepper.

"CHICKEN" AND VEGGIES

This healthy dish will allow you to grab an extra
scoop of cashew ice cream for dessert!

MAKES 2 SERVINGS

- 1 (10-ounce) bag frozen rice
- 1 (16-ounce) bag frozen vegetables (stir-fry mix or broccoli is best)
- 1 (8-ounce) bag vegan chicken strips
- Soy sauce, to taste

Cook the rice in the microwave according to the package directions and set aside. Cook the veggies in the microwave according to the package directions and set aside. Cook the chicken strips in the microwave until hot, about 1 ½ minutes, then chop into smaller pieces. Layer the rice, veggies, and chicken in a bowl, and top with soy sauce.

STEAMY RISOTTO-Y GOODNESS

Missing the comforts of home after a grueling
week of papers and exams? A nice steamy bowl
of ricey goodness will make you feel better,
even if Mom's not there to cook it for you.

— MAKES 4 SERVINGS —

- 3 cups hot veggie broth
- 1 teaspoon onion powder
- ½ teaspoon salt
- 1 pinch pepper
- 2 tablespoons olive oil
- 2 tablespoons vegan margarine
- 1 cup instant rice
- ¼ cup nutritional yeast

Combine the broth, onion powder, salt, and pepper and set aside. In a square baking dish or a glass pie plate, nuke the olive oil and margarine for 1 minute. Add the uncooked rice, stirring to coat with oil. Cover with a paper towel to prevent spattering and cook for 4 minutes. Pour the broth into the rice and stir. Nuke for 9 minutes. Stir again, then cook for another 9 minutes. Remove from the microwave and immediately stir in the nutritional yeast. Serve.

DRINKS

NOTE: THE FOLLOWING DRINKS ARE NOT THE KIND you'll find in a big metal barrel—they are the refreshing and delicious kind that won't make your head hurt the next day. Enjoy them as part of a meal or let them stand alone in all their glory.

DID YOU KNOW?

Despite the industry's claims, the evidence is clear that the animal protein in dairy products actually pulls calcium from the body. Population studies, including a groundbreaking Harvard study of more than 75,000 nurses, suggest that drinking cow's milk actually causes osteoporosis, given that the high acidity in milk erodes our bones. Alternatives to milk like soy, almond, rice, coconut, and flax milk are actually up to 50 percent higher in calcium and contain no cholesterol, growth hormones, antibiotics, or even pus (yuck!), like what is found in cow's milk.

FRUITY FRAT-TOOTIE SMOOTHIE

Sweeter than a blossoming frat boy bromance.

———————— MAKES 3 SERVINGS ————————

- 1 (16-ounce) can pineapple chunks
- 2 to 3 ripe bananas
- 1 (16-ounce) container frozen strawberries

Puree the pineapple, bananas, and strawberries in a blender until smooth.

INSTANT ENLIGHTEN-MINT CHOCOLATE LATTE

Screw finding your Zen—you need caffeine if you're going to make it to that damn 8:00 a.m. class.

—————— MAKES 1 SERVING ——————

- 1 cup chocolate soy milk
- 2 to 3 teaspoons instant coffee grounds
- ¼ teaspoon peppermint extract
- Sugar, to taste

Mix all the ingredients together and nuke until hot, about 2 minutes.

NO-EGG NOG

Ho, ho, ho, it's faux. Soy to the world! Okay, we're done.

MAKES 2 SERVINGS

- 2 cups soy milk
- 1 tablespoon instant vegan vanilla pudding powder
- ½ cup soy creamer
- ½ teaspoon vanilla extract
- ¼ teaspoon ground nutmeg
- ⅛ teaspoon rum extract
- ⅛ teaspoon salt

Combine 1 cup of soy milk and the instant pudding powder in a medium-size bowl, stirring until combined and thickened. Add the remaining milk and the creamer, mixing well. Stir in the vanilla, nutmeg, rum extract, and salt. Refrigerate overnight. Stir well before serving.

MELON-BERRY BLISS

This blissful treat is not only tasty, it's also chock-full of healthy, fruity goodness and perfect for breakfast when you don't have time to sit down and eat properly. It's so good for you, we're sure even your 'rents would approve.

MAKES 2 SERVINGS

- 2 frozen bananas (peeled and cut into chunks before freezing)
- 1 cup apple juice
- 1 cup frozen blueberries
- 4 to 5 cantaloupe chunks
- 4 to 5 honeydew chunks

Put all the ingredients in a blender and blend until smooth.

SPRING BREAK VIRGIN SMOOTHIE

This sweet and chilly little number is just
what you need to get yourself back on track
after a week of spring break debauchery.

—————— MAKES 1 SERVING ——————

- 1 frozen banana (peeled and cut into chunks before freezing)
- 4 frozen strawberries
- ¼ cup orange juice

Put all the ingredients in a blender and blend until smooth. Drink.

NUTTY PROFESSOR ALMOND LATTE

Highly caffeinated and slightly nutty, like that professor indigenous to all anthropology departments.

— MAKES 1 SERVING —

- 1 cup almond milk
- 2 to 3 teaspoons instant coffee crystals
- Sugar (optional)

Nuke the almond milk for 1 ½ minutes. Add the instant coffee crystals, making it as strong or as weak as you'd like. Sweeten with some sugar.

LATE NIGHT AT THE LIBERRY SOY SMOOTHIE

Packed full of protein and potassium, it's the perfect pick-me-up after a day spent nerding around the library.

──────── MAKES 1 SERVING ────────

- 1 cup soy milk
- 1 cup frozen raspberries or berry of your choice
- ½ frozen banana (peeled and cut into chunks before freezing)

Put all the ingredients into a blender and puree until smooth.

PUNK ROCK PUMPKIN SPICE LATTE

Sipping this seasonal delight while it's still hot? That is so punk rock.

— MAKES 1 TO 2 SERVINGS —

- 1 ½ cups almond milk
- 2 tablespoons canned pumpkin
- 2 tablespoons soy or almond creamer
- ½ to 1 tablespoon sugar
- 2 teaspoons vanilla extract
- ½ teaspoon pumpkin pie spice, plus more for garnish
- Instant coffee granules equivalent to 1 serving size

Mix the milk, pumpkin, and creamer together in a large bowl and then nuke for 1 minute. Add the sugar, vanilla extract, pumpkin pie spice, and instant coffee, and mix well. Nuke for about a minute more. Pour into one or two mugs (depending on mug size) and sprinkle a little more pumpkin pie spice on top.

PUN'KIN PIE SMOOTHIE

Forget the moo juice, pun'kin. The only dairy products you should have in your room are those crappy milk crates you're using for storage.

—— MAKES 1 SERVING ——

- 1 cup canned pumpkin
- 1 cup vanilla soy or almond milk
- 1 frozen banana (peeled and cut into chunks before freezing)
- 2 teaspoons pumpkin pie spice
- 5 ice cubes
- Sugar, to taste (optional)

Put all the ingredients—except the optional sugar—into a blender and blend until smooth. The frozen banana should give it some good sweetness, but feel free to add some sugar and blend a bit more.

CHOCOLATE CELEBRATION SHAKE

You've just finished your twenty-page psych paper. How will you celebrate? Shaking what your momma gave ya? You're delirious. Make yourself a chocolate shake instead.

MAKES 2 SERVINGS

- 4 cups frozen bananas (peeled and cut into chunks before freezing)
- 1 ½ cups soy or almond milk
- 3 tablespoons cocoa powder
- 2 tablespoons maple syrup
- 1 teaspoon vanilla

Thaw the frozen banana chunks for 5 to 10 minutes. Toss them and all of the other ingredients into a blender and blend until smooth. Serve immediately.

PARTY IN YOUR MOUTH PUNCH

Fizzy and festive even before someone spikes it.

—————— MAKES 4 SERVINGS ——————

- 2 (1-quart) bottles cranberry-apple juice
- 1 cup brown sugar
- 1 (1-quart) bottle ginger ale
- Orange slices, for garnish

Place the cranberry-apple juice and brown sugar in a large, microwavable dish and nuke for 3 minutes or until the sugar is dissolved. Chill in the refrigerator for at least an hour. Before serving, combine with the ginger ale in a punch bowl. Garnish with the orange slices.

SUCKY DAY STRAWBERRY SHAKE

Class sucked and your friends flaked. Treat yourself
to this sweet shake. You seriously deserve it.

MAKES 2 SERVINGS

- 6 strawberries, stems removed
- 1 tablespoon sugar
- 2 scoops vegan vanilla ice cream
- ½ cup soy milk

Sprinkle strawberries with sugar and let sit for a minute or so. Put
the ice cream, milk, and strawberries in a blender and blend until
smooth.

DIPS

A PARTY JUST ISN'T A PARTY UNLESS SOMEONE BRINGS the dip—or until a certain someone embarrasses himself by dancing really, really badly. Anyway, these little numbers won't leave anyone feeling bad about themselves the next day. And if you start whipping up these dips for parties, the invites you receive will quickly quadruple.

—— DID YOU KNOW? ——

It takes up to 10 pounds of grain to produce just one pound of meat. Sixty percent of the world's grain is fed to farmed animals, while millions of people worldwide will die from starvation this year.

PO PO'S PARTY
HEARTY SPINACH DIP

You know what they say—it's not a party without
dip and the cops showing up. We highly recommend
that first part. The second, not so much.

—————— MAKES 8 SERVINGS ——————

- 1 (10-ounce) box frozen chopped spinach
- 1 (12-ounce) container vegan sour cream
- ½ cup vegan mayonnaise
- 1 packet vegan onion soup mix
- 1 round loaf sourdough bread (or other round loaf)

Thaw the spinach in a bowl in the microwave for about 40 seconds on high. Using your hands, squeeze out all the water. Put the spinach in a dry bowl and stir in the sour cream, mayonnaise, and packet of onion soup mix. Let sit for a couple of hours, allowing the flavors to blend. Cut the top off the bread and scoop out the middle, making a bowl. Serve the dip in the bread bowl and cut the bread you scooped out into chunks for dipping.

FREUDIAN DIP

A therapeutic blend of beans, vegan sour cream, and salsa. Guaranteed to solve even the biggest of edible complexes.

―――――― MAKES 8 SERVINGS ――――――

- 1 (16-ounce) jar salsa
- 1 (15.5-ounce) can vegetarian refried beans
- 1 (12-ounce) container vegan sour cream
- Sliced jalapeños, to taste
- Tortilla chips

Mix all the ingredients, except the chips, together in a bowl and nuke for 2 minutes or until warm. Serve with tortilla chips.

CRAB-ULOUS DIP

Dive in—this flavorful vegan crab dip may be the closest you'll ever get to a semester at sea.

MAKES 8 SERVINGS

- 1 (12-ounce) can artichoke hearts, drained
- 12 ounces firm tofu, drained, patted dry, and mashed
- ½ cup vegan mayonnaise
- 1 tablespoon Old Bay seasoning, plus more to taste
- Crackers

Chop the artichoke hearts into small pieces and place in a bowl. Mix in the tofu, mayonnaise, and Old Bay seasoning. Nuke for 1 ½ minutes, checking to see if the top is slightly bubbly. If it's not, nuke for another 1 ½ minutes. Top with another sprinkle of Old Bay and serve warm with crackers.

SPIN ART DIP

Still better-looking than that stale macaroni art
you made when you were a kid—and tastier too.

—— MAKES 8 SERVINGS ——

- ½ (10-ounce) package frozen chopped spinach
- 1 (15-ounce) jar marinated artichoke hearts, drained but not rinsed
- 1 cup vegan mayonnaise
- ½ cup nutritional yeast (or substitute with vegan parmesan cheese)
- 1 teaspoon garlic powder
- Pepper, to taste
- 1 bag bagel chips

Defrost the spinach in the microwave by heating for about 40 seconds on high power, then squeeze out the excess water. Chop up the artichoke hearts. Mix all the ingredients except the bagel chips together in a bowl. Nuke for 3 minutes or until bubbly. Serve with bagel chips—and try not to eat all the dip yourself.

DARWIN'S DIP

A natural selection for that party you're planning. Do a couple of lunges though—it's all about survival of the fittest once this delish black bean dip hits the table.

—————— MAKES 8 SERVINGS ——————

- 1 (15-ounce) can black beans, drained and rinsed
- 1 cup salsa
- 1 tablespoon lemon juice
- 1 teaspoon onion powder

Mash beans with a fork. Add the salsa, lemon juice, and onion powder. Stir well and refrigerate 1 hour before serving.

SEVEN-LAYER MEXICAN DIP

Layer upon layer of yumminess. This dip is
deeper than your Philosophy 101 book.

===== MAKES 8 SERVINGS =====

- 1 (8-ounce) container vegan cream cheese
- ½ (1-ounce) packet taco seasoning
- 1 (15.5-ounce) can vegetarian refried beans
- 1 cup guacamole (store bought or see page 211)
- 1 cup chunky salsa
- 1 cup shredded lettuce
- 1 cup shredded vegan cheddar cheese
- 2 to 3 stalks green onion, chopped
- 1 bag tortilla chips

Mix the cream cheese and taco seasoning together. Spread onto
the bottom of a 9-inch pie plate or other dish. Layer the beans,
guacamole, salsa, lettuce, cheese, and green onions over the
cream cheese mixture. Cover and refrigerate for at least 1 hour.
Serve with tortilla chips.

CHOW DOWN CHILI-CHEEZ DIP

This "cheesy," spicy dip goes great with corn chips and will have everyone on your floor coming back for more.

MAKES 8 SERVINGS

- 1 (15-ounce) can vegan chili
- ½ cup shredded vegan cheddar cheese
- 1 tablespoon Mrs. Dash original seasoning
- Pepper, to taste
- 1 bag Fritos original corn chips

Put the chili, cheese, Mrs. Dash, and pepper into a big bowl and nuke for 2 minutes. Stir. Use Fritos for scooping.

CAMPUS STREAKER SAUSAGE DIP

Great for when you're on the run. Guaranteed
to turn any party into a sausage fest.

— MAKES 10 SERVINGS —

- 1 (14-ounce) tube vegan sausage
- 1 (15-ounce) can diced tomatoes with mild green chiles, drained
- 2 (8-ounce) containers vegan cream cheese, room temperature

Crumble the sausage as best you can and stir it into the tomatoes and cream cheese until evenly blended. Heat in the microwave for 3 minutes or until hot. Serve with tortilla chips.

CHEEZY BREEZY
BEAN DIP

Because you know that dried-up tray of nacho dip
stuff in the caf has been there since, like, 1992.

————— MAKES 4 SERVINGS —————

- 1 (14.5-ounce) can vegetarian refried beans
- 1 (8-ounce) can diced green chiles
- ¾ cup shredded vegan cheddar cheese

Put all the ingredients in a bowl, cover, and cook for about 2 minutes. Remove from the microwave and stir. Nuke for another minute or two. Stir again before serving with your fave chips.

UNHOLY GUACAMOLE

If the devil had a dip, this would be it.

—— MAKES 8 SERVINGS ——

- 3 large avocados, cut in half and pits removed
- 1 (16-ounce) jar salsa
- ¼ cup chopped cilantro
- Salt, to taste

Scoop the avocado flesh into a bowl. Add the salsa and cilantro and mix it all together. Season with salt. Serve with chips, on top of nachos, in burritos, or by itself.

FLOOR PARTY FOUR-LAYER BEAN DIP

Make up for your bad taste in late-night study music by charming your fellow dorm dwellers with an example of your good taste in food.

—————— MAKES 8 SERVINGS ——————

- 1 (15.5-ounce) can vegetarian refried beans
- 1 cup guacamole
- 1 (8-ounce) can diced tomatoes
- 1 (4.25-ounce) can chopped black olives
- 1 bag tortilla chips

Spread the can of beans on a large plate and nuke till warm. Top with the guac, then the tomatoes, and then the olives. Serve with chips!

AVO-CONTROL HUMMUS

Leave your self-control at the door
'cuz this dip don't play.

— MAKES 4 SERVINGS —

- 1 (15.5-ounce) can chickpeas, rinsed and drained
- 1 avocado, peeled and pitted
- 2 to 3 cloves garlic, minced (or ¼ teaspoon garlic powder)
- 1 teaspoon olive oil
- Salt, to taste
- Water
- 1 to 2 stalks green onion, chopped (optional)

Throw the chickpeas, avocado, garlic, olive oil, and salt into a blender. Add 2 tablespoons water and blend. Add more water and blend until you reach the desired consistency. Transfer the dip to a bowl and stir in green onions. Serve with chips, crackers, or veggies.

ORANGU-TANGY
ORANGE SPREAD

This sweet spread gets two opposable thumbs up.

―――――――――― MAKES 8 SERVINGS ――――――――――

- 1 (10-ounce) jar orange marmalade
- 1 (8-ounce) container vegan cream cheese, softened
- Crackers

Mix the orange marmalade with the vegan cream cheese in a bowl until well combined. Serve with crackers.

WOWY MAUI TROPICAL FRUIT SPREAD

This creamy coco-pine-orange concoction is hanging five in Hawaii, getting lei'd, and busting out the uke.

MAKES 8 SERVINGS

- 1 (8-ounce) can crushed pineapple, drained
- ½ (8-ounce) container vegan cream cheese, softened
- ½ cup canned mandarin oranges, drained
- ½ cup vegan sour cream
- 1 tablespoon coconut flakes (optional)

Mix everything together until well blended. Serve with crackers.

CHILLY DILLY SKINNY DIP

Great served with veggies and vegetarians
in the raw. So lose your drawers and hope
that the only thing chilly is the dip.

MAKES 8 SERVINGS

- 1 (12-ounce) container vegan sour cream
- 1 cup vegan mayonnaise
- 1 ½ teaspoons dried dill
- 1 teaspoon garlic powder
- 1 teaspoon onion powder
- 1 teaspoon salt

Stir everything together in a bowl and let chill in the refrigerator
for at least 1 hour. Serve with raw veggies or potato chips.

FIESTA IN YOUR MOUTH SALSA

*Not to be mistaken with a party in your pants—
unless you're into that type of thing.*

MAKES 8 SERVINGS

- 1 (28-ounce) can diced tomatoes, drained
- 1 (8-ounce) can diced green chiles, drained
- 1 (4.25-ounce) can diced black olives, drained
- ¼ cup distilled white vinegar
- ¼ cup olive oil
- 1 tablespoon dried chives
- 2 teaspoons garlic powder
- Salt, to taste

Mix all the ingredients together in a bowl and place in the fridge to chill for at least 1 hour. Stir before serving with corn tortilla chips.

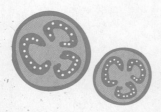

DORM ROOM 'SHROOM DIP

Even though these mushrooms aren't magic, your roommate must be trippin' if she thinks she's getting any of this delectable dip.

— MAKES 8 SERVINGS —

- ½ pound mushrooms, sliced
- 2 ½ tablespoons vegetable oil
- 2 teaspoons garlic powder
- 1 (8-ounce) container vegan cream cheese, softened
- 1 package vegan onion soup mix
- ⅛ teaspoon pepper
- 1 cup vegan sour cream
- 2 tablespoons vegan bacon bits
- Crackers

Combine the mushrooms, oil, and garlic powder in a bowl and nuke for 2 minutes or until the mushrooms are tender, stirring once. Add the cream cheese, soup mix, and pepper, and stir together thoroughly. Nuke again for 3 minutes, stirring frequently. Stir in the sour cream and the bacon bits. Nuke for 3 minutes or until heated through, stirring once. Serve with crackers.

SPRING BREAK TAHINI BIKINI DIP

Getting baked by the sun and playing in the ocean
all day can really take a lot out of you. After a
day at the beach, the last thing you want to do is
cook, so munch on this delicious dip instead.

MAKES 8 SERVINGS

- 1 cup salsa
- 1 cup tahini
- Tortilla chips

Mix the salsa and tahini together in a serving bowl. Serve with tortilla chips.

NACHO MOMMA'S CHEEZ DIP

Yo momma never made anything this good. Just sayin'.

MAKES 8 SERVINGS

- 1 (16-ounce) container salsa
- 1 (12-ounce) bag veggie burger crumbles
- 1 (12-ounce) container vegan sour cream
- 1 (10-ounce) block vegan nacho-style cheese, shredded

Mix everything together in a bowl and nuke for 5 minutes or until the crumbles are warm and the cheese is melted. Serve with tortilla chips.

CHEATER'S CHEESECAKE DIP

Cheating on tests? Bad idea. Pulling a fast one on your friends with this recipe? Great idea! They'll never know.

MAKES 8 SERVINGS

- 2 cups vegan marshmallow cream (Smucker's and Suzanne's Ricemellow Creme are good vegan options)
- 1 (8-ounce) container vegan cream cheese, softened

Cream the ingredients by mixing together slowly, then refrigerate for 30 minutes. Serve with fruit.

BROWN SUGAR
FUN DIP

Remember those "Fun Dip" packets from when you were a kid? You know, the candy dipping stick you'd dip into that crack-cocaine-like powder and lick until your head throbbed from the sugar? Well, think of this as Fun Dip's older, healthier cousin.

MAKES 4 SERVINGS

- 1 (8-ounce) container vegan cream cheese
- 2 tablespoons brown sugar

Stir together and serve with fresh fruit.

FEISTY FRUIT SALSA

Part sweet, part hot, just like your latest celeb crush.

MAKES 4 SERVINGS

- 1 (16-ounce) tub precut fruit of your choice
- 1 tablespoon fresh jalapeños, chopped (or use canned)
- 1 tablespoon lime juice
- 1 teaspoon chopped chives

Put all the ingredients into a bowl and mix well. Cover and chill for several hours or overnight.

NOTE:

If you have a toaster oven, make chips to serve with the fruit salsa by brushing flour tortillas with melted vegan margarine, then sprinkling with a mixture of cinnamon and sugar. Cut into wedges and bake at 350°F until crispy.

SNACKS

FEEL LIKE A TREAT? IS YOUR STOMACH GROWLING SO loudly you can hear it over your iPhone? Or do you just want to impress the people who keep wandering in and out of your room? These snacks are perfect for all those occasions, as well as between classes, on a study break, or late at night, when you're watching *Mean Girls* for the tenth time. They're fast, convenient, and have been known to help you miraculously make new friends with people down the hall or even on different floors. You know what we mean—all of a sudden everyone is your best friend when you have tasty-looking food.

DID YOU KNOW?

You can find vegan options at tons of chains, including Subway, Taco Bell, Johnny Rockets, P.F. Chang's, Chipotle, Denny's, Starbucks, Jamba Juice, Tropical Smoothie Café, zpizza, Panera Bread, Red Robin, White Castle, Yard House, and more!

SHAM "HAM" ROLL UPS

You've always wanted to make something with chives because they sound fancy—admit it.

MAKES 4 SERVINGS

- 1 (8-ounce) container vegan cream cheese
- 1 tablespoon chopped chives
- Salt and pepper, to taste
- 1 (5.5-ounce) package vegan ham deli slices

Mix the cream cheese, chives, salt, and pepper together. Spread the mixture on the deli slices and roll up. Use a toothpick to hold together.

QUICK CUKE ROLL UPS

For the love of humanities! Attendance is *not* optional in that philosophy class you're now late for. Eat this on the run and maybe you'll make it before your prof notices.

MAKES 1 TO 2 SERVINGS

- 1 large cucumber
- ½ to ¾ cup of your fave hummus (try the avocado hummus on page 213)

Carefully slice the cucumber into thin slices, lengthwise. If you have a vegetable peeler, it will work great—if not, a knife works just fine, but you'll have slightly thicker slices. Spread some hummus onto the top of each slice, then roll it up. Repeat until cucumber is gone. Hold each roll up together with a toothpick if you want to, but it's not necessary.

NOTE:

The Exclamation Point Eggless Salad on page 97 makes a great substitution for the hummus in this recipe.

WALKING TACO

Portable perfection that allows you to
walk and taco at the same time.

—————— MAKES 1 SERVING ——————

- 1 (1-ounce) bag corn chips (like Fritos)
- ¼ cup vegetarian refried beans
- 2 tablespoons guacamole
- 1 tablespoon salsa
- Handful of shredded vegan cheddar cheese (optional)

Cut open the bag of corn chips lengthwise. Spoon on the refried beans, guacamole, and salsa, and then sprinkle on the cheese. Eat!

PUMPKIN MUFFIN IN A MUG!

The good kind of muffin top.

───── MAKES 1 SERVING ─────

- 3 tablespoons flour
- 2 tablespoons brown sugar
- 1 tablespoon almond or soy milk
- 1 tablespoon canned pumpkin
- ½ tablespoon vegetable oil
- ½ tablespoon water
- ¼ teaspoon baking powder
- ⅛ teaspoon pumpkin pie spice
- Few pinches salt

Mix all the ingredients together well in a mug. Nuke for 1 to 2 minutes, until cooked through.

UNDERCOVER OINKERS

These "pigs in a blanket" aren't really pigs
at all, but we won't tell if you won't.

MAKES 8 SERVINGS

- 1 (12-ounce) package vegan veggie dogs
- Vegan cheese slices (optional)
- 1 (9-ounce) package vegan crescent rolls
- Your choice of condiments, for dipping

Roll up the veggie dogs (and cheese) in the crescent rolls. Oil a plate so the rolls won't stick to it, place the rolls on the plate, and heat in the microwave for 10 minutes or until fluffy.

BUFFALO CHICK'N TINDERS

Ahhh, love at first swipe. This spicy snack will heat things up with your hook-up and hold him over until the, er, main course.

MAKES 2 SERVINGS

- 1 (9-ounce) bag frozen vegan chicken strips (try Beyond Meat's lightly seasoned strips)
- 1 tablespoon vegan margarine
- ⅓ cup Frank's RedHot sauce

Dump the frozen chicken strips in a microwave-safe bowl and nuke for 2 to 3 minutes, until the strips are cooked. In a mug, nuke the margarine for about 15 seconds, until melted, then pour the hot sauce into the mug and stir to combine. Pour the sauce mixture over the chicken strips and stir to make sure every piece is coated. Nuke for another 10 to 15 seconds. Serve with vegan blue cheese dressing (try our recipe on page 141 or Follow Your Heart's dressing).

SLACKER SLAW

If you're too lazy to make this super-easy slaw,
we need to have a talk with your parents.

——— MAKES 4 SERVINGS ———

- ½ (16-ounce) bag coleslaw mix
- 2 tablespoons diced celery
- 1 tablespoon chopped chives
- ¼ cup vegan mayonnaise
- 2 teaspoons lemon juice
- Salt and pepper, to taste

Toss together the coleslaw mix, celery, and chives in a large bowl.
Add the mayonnaise and lemon juice and stir. Sprinkle with salt
and pepper. Refrigerate for at least 30 minutes before serving.

CHILI "NOT" DOGS

Bring these wieners to your next sausage—er, soysage—party and watch 'em disappear.

MAKES 1 SERVING

- 1 vegan veggie dog
- 1 hot dog bun
- ¼ cup canned vegan chili
- Mustard, to taste
- Dill relish, to taste (optional)

Cook the veggie dog according to the package directions. Place in the bun and top with the chili, mustard, and dill relish. Serve with onion rings or french fries.

ONE-BITE PIZZAS

Downing an entire beer in one breath? Big
deal. Now you can brag to your buddies that
you can take out a whole pizza in one bite.

MAKES 6 SERVINGS

- 1 (12-ounce) bag veggie burger crumbles
- 1 (14-ounce) jar pizza sauce
- 1 bag mini bagels, toasted
- 1 cup shredded vegan mozzarella cheese

Put the crumbles in a bowl, and nuke for 2 to 3 minutes or until warm. Take out of the microwave and mix in the pizza sauce. Spoon onto the bagels, top with the cheese, and nuke for 1 minute or until the cheese is melted.

GARLIC CAULIFLOWER MASH

Quick and easy comfort food from the
discomfort of your cramped kitchen.

── MAKES 2 SERVINGS ──

- 1 (12-ounce) bag cauliflower florets (not frozen)
- 1 to 2 tablespoons original almond or soy milk
- 1 to 2 tablespoons vegan margarine
- ½ teaspoon garlic powder
- Salt and pepper, to taste

Cook the cauliflower florets in the microwave according to directions on the bag. Dump the florets into a large, microwave-safe bowl, then mash with a fork. Add the milk, margarine, garlic powder, salt, and pepper, and mix well. Nuke for another 30 seconds, then serve.

OYSTER CRACKER SNACKERS

So good you can't just have one.

MAKES 4 SERVINGS

- ¾ cup olive oil
- 1 teaspoon salt
- ½ teaspoon garlic powder, plus more to taste
- ½ teaspoon onion powder, plus more to taste
- 1 (24-ounce) bag oyster crackers

Mix the oil, salt, garlic powder, and onion powder together in a small bowl. Place the crackers on a rimmed baking sheet and pour the oil mixture over the crackers, sprinkling them with more garlic powder and onion powder. Let sit for 10 minutes, mix, then let sit for an additional 20 minutes. Mix again and eat.

CHEEZY MOVIE POPCORN

You need a break. Turn off your brain, make this snack, and love/hate-watch a Lifetime movie.

— MAKES 2 SERVINGS —

- 1 bag vegan microwavable popcorn
- 2 tablespoons vegan margarine
- 2 tablespoons nutritional yeast
- Salt, to taste

Microwave popcorn according to directions, then open the bag to let the popped popcorn start to cool. In a mug, nuke the margarine until melted, about 20 seconds or so. Pour the margarine into the bag of popcorn, then add in the nutritional yeast and salt. Close the top of the bag and shake well until everything is well mixed. Eat right out of the bag or dump the popcorn into a bowl to serve.

SHUCKIN' AWESOME CORN ON THE COB

A delicious meal and, if you're feeling crafty,
a chance to be the only guy on campus rocking
a corncob pipe. Everyone knows that ladies
can't resist a corncob pipe. How do you think
Mark Twain got all the ladies' attention?

MAKES 2 SERVINGS

- 2 ears of corn, still in the husk
- Salt, pepper, and vegan margarine, to taste

Pop the ears of corn in the microwave and nuke for 8 minutes. Using oven mitts or other hand protection, remove the corn from the microwave and then shuck the corn. Put the shucked corn on a plate and top with salt, pepper, and margarine, or just eat it plain.

LEMONY CARROTS

And meat eaters say that vegetarians
only eat rabbit food. Oh, wait...

MAKES 4 SERVINGS

- ½ (10-ounce) bag baby carrots
- 1 tablespoon vegan margarine
- 1 tablespoon lemon juice, or more to taste
- Salt and pepper, to taste

Arrange the carrots in a single layer on a plate and dot with margarine. Cover and nuke for 6 minutes or until almost tender. Sprinkle with lemon juice and season with salt and pepper.

POOR MAN'S PIZZAS

Ivy-league eating on a community-college budget.

— MAKES 4 SERVINGS —

- 🌿 24 crackers of your choice
- 🌿 ¼ cup pizza sauce
- 🌿 24 slices vegan pepperoni or other "meat" topping of your choice
- 🌿 1 ½ cups finely shredded vegan mozzarella cheese

Top each cracker with some pizza sauce, pepperoni or other meat, and vegan cheese. Microwave for 1 minute or until the cheese is melted.

HAPPY TRAILZ MIX

Great for grazing a trail across campus.

──── MAKES 4 SERVINGS ────

- 1 vegan chocolate bar, broken apart
- ½ cup corn-puff cereal (try Corn Pops or Kix)
- ½ cup mixed nuts
- ¼ cup coconut flakes (optional)
- ¼ cup dried pineapple
- ¼ cup mini pretzels
- ¼ cup raisins

Mix all the ingredients together.

PIZZA FUN-DO

Totally doable cheezy fondue that will
leave your friends swooning.

MAKES 4 SERVINGS

- 3 cups shredded vegan mozzarella cheese
- 2 (10-ounce) cans pizza sauce
- 1 (12-ounce) bag veggie burger crumbles
- 1 teaspoon garlic powder
- 1 teaspoon onion powder
- Cubed French bread

Mix the cheese, pizza sauce, crumbles, and garlic and onion powders in a large, microwave-safe bowl. Nuke, uncovered, for 6 minutes or until the cheese melts. Stir to blend. Serve with bread cubes to dip into the fondue.

CAULIFLOWER POWER FLORETS

Dig that Dijon.

MAKES 4 SERVINGS

- 1 (14-ounce) bag frozen cauliflower florets
- ½ cup vegan mayonnaise
- ¼ cup Dijon mustard
- 1 cup shredded vegan cheddar cheese

Put the cauliflower in a bowl and nuke for 5 minutes or until warm. Remove from the microwave. In another bowl, mix the mayonnaise and the mustard. Spoon onto the cauliflower and top with the cheese. Nuke for an additional 2 minutes or until the cheese is melted.

STUFFED AVO-CUDDLES

Like you, these avocadoes were made to be spooned.

============== MAKES 2 SERVINGS ==============

- ½ (8.75-ounce) can whole-kernel corn
- 8 to 10 cherry tomatoes, cut in half
- 1 large avocado
- Salt, pepper, and garlic powder, to taste

Mix together the corn and tomato halves in a bowl. Cut the avocado in half lengthwise and remove the pit. Scoop out a little more of the avocado so you'll have a larger space for the filling. Chop up the avocado that you scooped out and stir it into the corn mixture, then season with salt, pepper, and garlic powder. Season the avocado halves with salt and pepper, then spoon the corn mixture into the avocados.

PANCAKE PIZZA

You already start the day at the crack of noon; you might as well combine lunch with breakfast too.

MAKES 1 SERVING

- 1 cup vegan pancake mix
- ½ cup original soy milk
- 1 ½ teaspoons egg replacer mixed with 2 tablespoons water
- ½ (8-ounce) can black olives, sliced
- ½ (8-ounce) can mushrooms, pieces and stems
- ½ cup shredded vegan mozzarella cheese
- Pizza sauce, to taste

Mix together the pancake mix, soy milk, and egg-replacer mixture in a small bowl. Stir until blended. Add the olives, mushrooms, and cheese. Microwave for 2 minutes or until solid. Top with pizza sauce and enjoy.

STADIUM CORN DOGS

Feel free to put these on a stick to get the experience
of the game from the comfort of your room.

————— MAKES 4 SERVINGS —————

- 1 cup all-purpose flour
- 1 cup cornmeal
- 1 tablespoon baking powder
- 1 teaspoon salt
- 1 cup original soy milk
- ⅓ cup canola oil
- 1 teaspoon egg replacer mixed with ¼ cup of water
- 4 vegan veggie dogs, sliced
- Ketchup and mustard, for dipping

Put the dry ingredients (flour, cornmeal, baking powder, and salt) in one bowl and mix. Put the wet ingredients (soy milk, oil, and egg replacer) in another bowl and mix. Combine the wet and dry ingredients into a square casserole dish and mix until smooth. Plop the veggie dogs in the mixture equal distance apart and pop the dish in the microwave. Nuke on high for 5 to 6 minutes or until the surface appears dry, rotating the dish after 2 to 3 minutes. Let stand 5 minutes before serving. Cut into squares, and serve with ketchup and mustard for dipping.

NO-PAN CROUTONS

Delicious with salad or on their own, and way better
than those crusty, little bricks they serve at the caf.

MAKES 4 SERVINGS

- ¼ cup vegan margarine
- 2 teaspoons garlic powder
- 1 teaspoon salt
- 4 cups French bread, cut into ¾-inch cubes

Put the margarine in a bowl and nuke for 1 minute or until melted.
Stir in the garlic and salt. Add the bread cubes, stirring gently to
coat. Microwave on high for 4 ½ to 5 minutes, stopping it to stir
2 or 3 times. Let cool. Store in an airtight container. (The croutons
will crisp as they cool.)

COMFORTING CORNBREAD

Comfort food for those blustery days...when
one of your profs gets a little long-winded.

─── MAKES 6 SERVINGS ───

- ½ cup cornmeal
- ½ cup flour
- ½ cup original almond or soy milk
- 2 ½ tablespoons sugar
- 1 egg replacer (1 ½ teaspoons Ener-G Egg
  Replacer mixed well with 2 tablespoons water)
- 2 tablespoons vegetable oil
- 2 teaspoons baking powder
- ¼ teaspoon salt

Mix all the ingredients together in a microwave-safe glass bowl. Heat in the microwave on high 3 minutes or until a toothpick or knife inserted into the center comes out clean. Delicious served with chili!

SLAYER'S SLICE

One taste and you can ward off any campus
vampires simply by breathing on them.

———— MAKES 2 SERVINGS ————

- 2 rolls of any kind, cut in half (burger buns, hot dogs buns, dinner rolls, etc.), toasted
- Olive oil
- Garlic salt
- Dried oregano or parsley

Brush the sliced side of the toasted rolls with a little olive oil (don't soak it, but make sure the surface is covered). Sprinkle with a little garlic salt and dried oregano or parsley. Nuke in the microwave for 15 seconds.

EXTRA CREDIT
"HAM" TOAST POINTS

Zero percent effort; 110 percent satisfacción.

— MAKES 8 SERVINGS —

- 1 (5.5-ounce) package vegan ham deli slices
- 1 ½ cups vegan mayonnaise
- ½ cup shredded vegan cheddar cheese
- ½ cup vegan parmesan cheese
- 1 teaspoon garlic powder
- ½ teaspoon onion powder
- 1 large loaf Italian bread

Tear apart the slices of ham, then mix them in a bowl with the mayo, cheeses, garlic powder, and onion powder. Slice and toast the bread; when toasted, top with a spoonful of the spread. Pop in the microwave until the cheese is melted.

FRANKIE'S FARTS

Not a good meal to eat before a date, an exam, or pretty much any situation where others will be trapped in close proximity to you, but delicious nonetheless! Our apologies to your roommate.

MAKES 2 SERVINGS

- 1 (15.5-ounce) can vegetarian baked beans
- 2 vegan veggie dogs

Pour the beans into a microwave-safe bowl. Slice the veggie dogs and mix them into the beans. Nuke for 3 minutes and eat.

GOLIVE HARDEN BRUSCHETTA

Like the good stuff at that Italian place, without the crying babies and jacked-up prices.

MAKES 2 SERVINGS

- 1 (14.5-ounce) can diced tomatoes, drained
- 1 (2.25-ounce) can chopped black olives, drained
- 2 tablespoons olive oil
- 2 teaspoons balsamic vinegar (or less for a milder flavor)
- Garlic powder, to taste
- Salt and pepper, to taste
- 2 whole wheat pita breads

Put the tomatoes and olives in a bowl and mix together. Add the olive oil and balsamic vinegar and stir, mixing well. Season with garlic powder, salt, and pepper. Toast the pita in the toaster. Tear into smaller pieces. Dip into the tomato mixture, scooping some of the olives and tomatoes, and eat!

EZ CHEEZY BROCCOLEEZY

No, nutritional yeast is not a malady caused by malnutrition. It's a delicious cheese alternative best when served smothered on broccoli. 'Nuff said.

MAKES 2 SERVINGS

- 1 (10-ounce) bag frozen broccoli florets
- ¼ cup nutritional yeast
- Salt, to taste
- 2 tablespoons vegan margarine

Nuke the broccoli for 4 minutes. Set aside. Mix the nutritional yeast and salt together, and sprinkle onto the broccoli. Add the margarine and nuke for 1 minute. Stir together and eat!

DON'T GET CREAMED SPINACH

Let's face it. That inadvertent bicep curl you
do when you bring your fork to your mouth is
as close as you're going to get to pumping iron.
Better load up on as much spinach as you can.

MAKES 2 SERVINGS

- ¾ cup original soy milk
- 2 tablespoons flour
- 2 tablespoons vegan margarine
- ¼ teaspoon salt
- Pepper, to taste
- 1 (10-ounce) package frozen spinach, thawed

Mix together everything but the spinach and nuke for 30 seconds.
Stir. Heat again for 30 seconds. Stir again. Add the thawed spinach
and nuke for 1 minute. Stir and eat.

"AGE OF ASPARAGUS" SPEARS

Dig the far-out flavor, man. This steamy veggie is
guaranteed to get you some hippie-chick love.

MAKES 2 SERVINGS

- ½ pound fresh asparagus, woody ends trimmed or snapped off
- 3 to 4 tablespoons olive oil
- 2 teaspoons red wine vinegar
- Salt and black pepper, to taste
- 2 to 3 tablespoons chopped walnuts

Nuke the asparagus for 2 to 3 minutes, until crisp but tender. While it's cooking, whisk together the oil, vinegar, salt, and pepper. To serve, drizzle the vinaigrette over the asparagus and garnish with the chopped walnuts.

BOOZY BEER BREAD

The bad news is that it won't slide through your
beer bong. The good news is you can seriously
eat about twenty loaves of this beer-soaked bread
before someone wrestles your car keys from you.

MAKES 8 SERVINGS

- ⅓ cup cornflake crumbs
- 2 cups self-rising flour
- 1 cup all-purpose flour
- 3 tablespoons sugar
- 12 ounces beer, regular or nonalcoholic,
  at room temperature
- 1 tablespoon vegan margarine, softened

Spray a glass loaf pan with cooking spray, then sprinkle the
bottom and sides with half the cornflake crumbs. Mix the flours,
sugar, and beer together to make the batter. Spoon the batter
into the pan and top with the margarine, making sure the top is
evenly coated. Top with the remaining cornflake crumbs. Nuke
on medium heat for 9 minutes, then on high heat for 2 minutes.

FANCY PANTS GREEN BEANS

Spicy as an Argentine salsa on that TV dance show
you'll never admit you like, but much more appetizing
then the "manitards" the contestants wear.

— MAKES 4 SERVINGS —

- 1 (14.5-ounce) can French-style green beans, drained
- 1 tablespoon salsa
- 1 tablespoon vegan margarine
- ½ teaspoon spicy sesame oil

Mix everything together in a bowl and nuke for about 1 ½ minutes, until hot.

FRIENDS WITH BENNIES BAKED BEANS

An easy and fulfilling recipe you don't have to commit a lot of time or energy to—much like that FWB thing you've got going on.

MAKES 4 SERVINGS

- 1 (16-ounce) can red kidney beans, drained
- 1 (16-ounce) can vegetarian baked beans, undrained
- ½ cup chunky style salsa
- 1 teaspoon onion powder
- 1 teaspoon yellow mustard

Combine all the ingredients in a bowl and mix well. Cover with microwave-safe wax paper and nuke for 5 minutes or until the flavors are blended, stirring twice during cooking.

MUY CALIENTE CORN

Being set up by a friend? Cook this to impress your date. At least if the date's not hot, the corn will be.

——— MAKES 4 SERVINGS ———

- 1 (14-ounce) can corn, drained
- 1 (7-ounce) can diced jalapeños, drained
- 1 (4-ounce) jar pimentos
- 2 tablespoons vegan margarine
- 1 teaspoon onion powder
- Salt and pepper, to taste

Combine the corn, jalapeños, pimentos, margarine, and onion powder in a microwave-safe bowl. Cover and nuke for 4 minutes or until hot, stirring every minute or so. Add salt and pepper and eat.

TROPICAL LOVE TRIANGLES

Polynesian-inspired toast points as sweet and
satisfying as any tropical delight you can imagine
but without the hassle of getting a passport.

MAKES 4 SERVINGS

- 8 slices of your favorite bread
- 1 (15-ounce) can tomato sauce
- 1 (5.5-ounce) package vegan ham deli slices
- 1 (14-ounce) can pineapple, crushed and drained
- 1 ¼ cup shredded vegan mozzarella cheese

Cut crusts off bread. Toast the bread and cut each piece in half diagonally, so you have two triangles. Spread the tomato sauce on each slice. Tear up a slice of ham and place it on top of the toast. Sprinkle the pineapple on the toast and top with vegan cheese. Repeat process for each piece of toast. Pop in the microwave for 30 seconds or until cheese is melted.

STUFFED 'SHROOMS

Stuffed to the top and packed full of crumbs. Like your side of the room—but much more tastefully done.

— MAKES 4 SERVINGS —

- ½ pound medium-size mushrooms, washed, with stems removed and saved
- ½ cup chopped chives
- ¼ cup vegan margarine
- 3 tablespoons vegan breadcrumbs

Arrange the mushroom caps, hollow-side up, in a single layer in a baking dish. Set aside. Chop up the mushroom stems and combine with the chives and margarine in another dish. Nuke, uncovered, for 3 to 4 minutes, stirring twice. Add the breadcrumbs, stir, and set aside. Cover the mushroom caps and nuke for 2 to 3 minutes or until nearly cooked, rotating the dish a half turn after the first minute. Stuff each cap with some of the breadcrumb mixture. Cover and nuke for 2 minutes or until hot.

SPINACH LIMÓN

It's like the liquor: flavorful, fresh, and delicious, except you can't get arrested for carrying this in an open container.

MAKES 2 SERVINGS

- 1 (10-ounce) bag fresh spinach, rinsed
- 2 ½ tablespoons vegan margarine
- 1 tablespoon lemon juice
- 1 teaspoon garlic powder
- Salt and pepper, to taste

Put the spinach in a serving dish. Add the margarine, lemon juice, and garlic. Cover with plastic wrap. Nuke for about 2 minutes or until the margarine is melted and the spinach is wilted. Remove the plastic wrap and eat.

SPOTLIGHT ON: POTATOES

THERE ARE THOUSANDS OF VARIETIES OF POTATOES and just as many ways to prepare them. This is definitely a good thing, since potatoes are delicious and filling. They're also a great defense weapon (who would ever expect you to throw a potato at them?)—but that's beside the point. Potatoes are quick, tasty, and easy to make, so be sure to always keep some on hand.

DID YOU KNOW?

Animal agriculture contributes more greenhouse gases than all transportation in the world combined. If every American skipped eating one meal of chicken per week and ate vegan food instead, it would be like taking more than 500,000 cars off the road. Going vegan would decrease your carbon footprint significantly and is the greenest thing you can do!

NOTE:

When a recipe calls for more than one potato, try to find potatoes about the same size for even cooking.

GERMAN 'TATO SALAD

Even if you can't get to the beer garden, you
can be an honorary German year-round with
this tasty concoction of taters and mustard.

MAKES 4 SERVINGS

- 2 pounds red potatoes
- 1 cup vegan bacon bits
- ½ cup chopped chives
- 6 tablespoons vinegar, or to taste
- ⅓ cup vegetable oil
- 3 tablespoons brown mustard, or to taste
- Salt and pepper, to taste

Wash the potatoes and stab them with a fork (to vent). Cook in the microwave for 5 minutes or until tender. You should be able to easily stick a fork in them, but they shouldn't fall apart. Allow to cool for a bit, then cut into cubes. Mix together the bacon bits, chives, vinegar, oil, and mustard in a large bowl. Toss the potatoes into the bowl and mix until the potatoes are well coated. Add salt and pepper.

CLASSIC POTATO SALAD FAKE OUT

With vegan mayo instead of the eggy original, no one will ever guess that their new favorite classic potato salad is a faker.

MAKES 4 SERVINGS

- 4 large russet or Idaho potatoes
- 1 cup chopped celery
- 1 cup vegan mayonnaise
- ½ cup chopped chives
- 1 teaspoon Dijon mustard
- Salt and pepper, to taste

Wash the potatoes and stab them with a fork (to vent). Cook in the microwave for 8 minutes or until tender. You should be able to stick a fork in them, but they shouldn't fall apart. Allow to cool for a bit, then cut into cubes. Mix together the celery, mayonnaise, chives, and mustard. Add the potatoes and toss until well coated. Add salt and pepper. Chill for one hour and serve.

TOUGH AND STUFFED SWEET POTATOES

Sweet potatoes as stuffed with attitude as your boyfriend's ex, only this dish won't give you the stink eye.

MAKES 4 SERVINGS

- 4 medium sweet potatoes
- 1 (15-ounce) can black beans, drained
- 1 (10-ounce) can diced tomatoes
- 1 tablespoon vegetable oil
- ¾ teaspoon salt
- ¼ cup vegan sour cream

Wash the sweet potatoes and stab them with a fork in several places to vent. Nuke in the microwave until tender all the way to the center, 12 to 15 minutes, then take out and let cool. Meanwhile, in a medium bowl, mix together the beans, tomatoes, oil, and salt. Nuke for about 2 to 3 minutes, until just heated through. When just cool enough to handle, cut each sweet potato lengthwise (being careful not to cut all the way through), press open to make a well in the center, and spoon the bean mixture into the well. Top with the sour cream.

TEACHER'S PET TATER SKINS

Lay it on thick and hang on every bite. We promise, the Bac*Os are as fake-o as your interest in what the teacher is actually saying.

--- MAKES 1 SERVING ---

- 1 Idaho potato
- ¼ cup shredded vegan cheddar cheese
- 1 tablespoon vegan bacon bits
- 2 tablespoons vegan sour cream
- Salt and pepper, to taste

Wash the potato and stab it with a fork multiple times, like a blond in a bad horror flick. Nuke on high for 5 minutes or until tender. Take out of the microwave, allow to cool for 1 to 2 minutes, and cut in half. Top with the cheese and bacon bits. Put back in the microwave and nuke for another minute. Take out and top with the sour cream, salt, and pepper.

THE SWEETNESS
TATER SALAD

Next to bringing a cooler full of "refreshing beverages,"
bringing this surprisingly sweet tater salad to your next
picnic is the easiest way to score points with your pals.

—————— MAKES 2 SERVINGS ——————

- 1 (16-ounce) bag coleslaw mix (shredded cabbage)
- ½ (20-ounce) can diced pineapple, undrained
- ½ (10-ounce) bag shredded carrots
- 1 sweet potato, peeled and grated
- 1 apple, cored and diced
- ¼ cup lemon juice
- ¼ cup olive oil
- Handful of raisins

Toss all the ingredients together in a large bowl and serve
immediately.

PIONEER POTATO SALAD

Tastes like your hundred-year-old granny's
two-hundred-year-old recipe.

--- MAKES 4 SERVINGS ---

- 2 to 3 medium potatoes
- ½ cup vegan mayonnaise
- 2 teaspoons garlic powder
- 1 teaspoon pepper
- Dill relish, to taste

Wash the potatoes, stab them with a fork, and nuke for about 3 minutes. Flip the potatoes over (careful, they're hot!) and nuke for another 3 minutes. Mix the mayo, spices, and relish in a medium-size bowl. Let the potatoes rest in the microwave for a few minutes (they will continue to cook). Remove the potatoes and cut into bite-size pieces—usually halves and then eighths will do—carefully, as they may still be hot inside. Mix the potatoes with the sauce and enjoy!

POTATOES IN PARADISE

*Single White Potato meets Dicey Green Avocado...
you know this can only end with the two of them
wrapping up in a tortilla and getting freaky.*

———— MAKES 1 SERVING ————

- 1 Yukon gold potato
- 1 avocado, diced
- ½ cup shredded lettuce
- Salt and pepper, to taste
- 1 (10-inch) tortilla

Wash the potato and stab it several times with a fork to vent (and get your frustrations out). Nuke for about 6 minutes or until soft but not mushy. Cut into small cubes once cooled, mix with the avocado, and season with salt and pepper. Nuke the tortilla for 10 seconds to soften. Toss the potato mixture and lettuce onto the tortilla and wrap up.

DEVILED POTATOES

When you're having the week from hell, treat yo'self to these taters.

─────── MAKES 10 TO 12 SERVINGS ───────

- 5 to 6 small yellow potatoes
- ½ block extra-firm tofu
- ¼ cup vegan mayonnaise
- 2 teaspoons yellow mustard
- 1 teaspoon water

- ½ teaspoon dried dill
- ½ teaspoon garlic powder
- ½ teaspoon turmeric
- ¼ teaspoon salt, plus more for sprinkling
- Pepper, to taste
- Paprika, to taste (optional)

Stab each potato a few times with a fork, then microwave, two at a time, on a plate for 4 to 5 minutes, until the potatoes are soft enough that you can easily cut them with a knife. Let them cool a bit, then cut each potato in half lengthwise and allow to cool completely. You can stick them in the fridge for a while to speed up the process. In the meantime, in a blender, crumble the tofu, then add the mayo, yellow mustard, water, dill, garlic powder, turmeric, salt, and pepper, and blend until well combined. Taste and adjust spices if needed. Once the potato halves are cool, use a spoon to scoop out a bit of the potato, so there's a good-size roundish space in the potato for the filling, then sprinkle the halves with some salt. Use a spoon (or a small cookie scoop if you are lucky enough to have one!) to put some of the tofu filling in each potato—enough so that the filling is piled up a bit on top of the potato. Sprinkle with a bit more dill and some paprika.

PRETTY MUCH THE BEST BURRITO

It's a Tatorito—a potato and a burrito mixed together. Get it?

=== MAKES 2 SERVINGS ===

- 1 sweet potato
- 1 (15-ounce) can pinto beans, drained and rinsed
- 2 large tortillas
- ½ cup salsa verde
- 2 tablespoons guacamole or vegan sour cream (or both, if you're feelin' feisty)

Wash the sweet potato and poke some holes in it with a fork. Nuke on high for 5 to 6 minutes or until softened. Remove from the microwave, allow to cool for two minutes, cut into small cubes, and set aside. Nuke the beans in a microwave-safe dish for 2 minutes. One at a time, nuke the tortillas for 10 seconds to soften. To make the burritos, put half the potato cubes and half the beans in the middle of each tortilla. Top each with half of the salsa and half of the guacamole or sour cream. Eat.

LAZY MAN'S CANDIED YAMS

Just like your mama's home cooking if your mama were too lazy to actually cook. We won't slap you for eating it with your fingers, but you do have to get off your ass and cook it yourself.

MAKES 1 SERVING

- 1 sweet potato
- 1 tablespoon maple syrup, or to taste

Wash the sweet potato and poke it with a fork multiple times to vent. Nuke on high for 5 minutes or until tender. Let cool. Then pick up the sweet 'tato, squirt it with some maple syrup, and eat it like an apple.

IDAHO? NO, *YOU* DA HO'
Potatoes au gratin

Stop fighting with your roommate and agree
to disagree over this glorious au gratin.

MAKES 2 SERVINGS

- 2 medium potatoes, washed and sliced
- ½ cup nutritional yeast
- ½ cup original soy milk
- 1 teaspoon garlic powder
- 1 teaspoon
- Salt, to taste

Put the potato slices in a bowl and nuke for 3 minutes. Mix the remaining ingredients together until a sauce is formed. Top the potatoes with the sauce and microwave for 2 to 3 minutes or until the potatoes are tender.

TWICE-NUKED POTATO

Finally—something more baked than your roommate.

MAKES 1 SERVING

- 1 medium baking potato
- ⅓ cup shredded vegan cheddar cheese
- ¼ cup vegan sour cream
- 1 teaspoon chopped chives
- Salt, pepper, and garlic powder, to taste

Wash the potato and stab it with a fork like it owes you money. Nuke for 5 minutes or until potato is tender. Remove from the microwave, and when cool enough to handle, cut in half lengthwise. Use a large spoon to scoop out the inside of the potato into a bowl, leaving the skin intact. Stir the cheese, sour cream, and chives into the scooped-out part of the potato. Season with salt, pepper, and garlic powder, and mix well. Nuke for 2 to 3 minutes or until heated through. Scoop the mixture back into the potato skin and eat.

'TIS THE SEASON(ED) POTATO WEDGES

Look, dude, it may not be winter, but try these anyway!

— MAKES 4 SERVINGS —

- ¾ cup vegan margarine, melted
- 4 to 6 small potatoes, washed and cut into thick wedges
- Garlic-and-herb seasoning salt, to taste

Nuke the margarine in a small bowl until melted, about 90 seconds. Put the potato wedges on a microwave-safe plate and pour the melted margarine on top, making sure that each wedge is well coated. Sprinkle the seasoned salt over the wedges and nuke for about 2 minutes or until tender. Let cool before eating.

PIZ-TATO

This super-simple pizza/potato combo will be
ready to devour before you can speed-dial the pizza
delivery guy. Besides, isn't it just a bit shameful
that you two are on a first-name basis?

MAKES 1 SERVING

- 1 large baking potato
- 3 tablespoons pizza sauce
- ⅓ cup shredded vegan mozzarella cheese
- Vegan pepperoni, black olives, or other pizza toppings (optional)

Wash the potato and stab it with a fork like you mean it. Microwave for about 6 minutes or until squishy when lightly squeezed. Cut the potato in half and spoon pizza sauce over each half. Top with vegan cheese and toppings, and pop back into the microwave for another minute or until the cheese is melted.

CHEATER TATERS AND ONIONS

Whipping up a bowl of these taters and onions is even easier than paying the nerdy freshman downstairs to write your research paper.

— MAKES 1 SERVING —

- 1 potato, washed and sliced
- ½ small onion, sliced
- 2 tablespoons vegan margarine
- Salt and pepper, to taste

Put all the ingredients in a bowl. Cover and nuke for 4 minutes or until the potatoes are tender.

MICROECONOMICAL MICROWAVE POTATOES

When your supplies cannot meet your demands, there are always potatoes—cheap, filling, and delicious.

MAKES 4 SERVINGS

- 3 large potatoes, peeled and cubed
- 2 tablespoons vegan margarine
- 1 teaspoon onion powder
- 1 teaspoon garlic powder
- ½ teaspoon salt
- ⅛ teaspoon pepper

Combine all the ingredients in a dish and nuke for about 1 minute, until the margarine melts. Stir. Cook for 10 minutes more, stirring occasionally.

BEN FRANKLIN'S MISERLY MASHERS

When tuition's due, it's all about the Benjamins. Make your cash go further with these penny-pinching potatoes.

——— MAKES 4 SERVINGS ———

- 4 servings instant vegan mashed potatoes
- 1 tablespoon chopped chives
- 1 tablespoon vegan sour cream
- Handful of shredded vegan cheddar cheese
- Salt and pepper, to taste
- 1 tablespoon vegan bacon bits

Cook the instant potatoes according to the package directions. Mix together with the chives, sour cream, cheese, salt, and pepper. It's best to add the bacon bits right before serving. There you go!

SCHOLAR-CHIPS

You so earned these crunchy munchies.

MAKES 1 SERVING

- 1 tablespoon vegetable oil
- 1 Idaho potato, washed and sliced paper thin (use the "cheese slice" part of a grater to do this)
- Salt, to taste

Pour the oil into a plastic bag (a produce bag works well). Add the potato slices and shake to coat. Lightly coat a large dinner plate with oil. Arrange the potato slices in a single layer on the plate. Nuke for 3 to 5 minutes or until lightly browned. Place the chips in a bowl and toss with salt. Let cool. Eat.

DESSERTS

IF YOU'RE ANYTHING LIKE US, YOU HAVE AN OUT-OF-control sweet tooth that can flare up anytime, anywhere. It demands attention like a drunk guy at a party. Well, now you can satisfy yourself with some Screaming Pudding Pie or No-Bake Chocolate Cake. Feel free to share to score some brownie points with your RA.

DID YOU KNOW?

According to the American Dietetic Association, "Well-planned vegan and other types of vegetarian diets are appropriate for all stages of the life cycle, including during pregnancy, lactation, infancy, childhood, and adolescence."

284

STRAWBERRY
PLEASECAKE BITES

All the deliciousness of strawberry cheesecake in a quick bite!

=== MAKES 8 BITES ===

- 1 pound strawberries
- 1 (8-ounce) container vegan cream cheese
- 1 ½ cups powdered sugar
- 1 teaspoon vanilla extract
- 1 vegan graham cracker, or a handful of animal crackers

Remove the strawberry stems, carving a hollow spot as you do, then slice a tiny piece off each strawberry tip, so the strawberries will stand up. Be careful not to cut off too much, since you don't want the cheesecake mixture to leak through the bottoms. Combine the cream cheese, powdered sugar, and vanilla extract, and beat until nice and fluffy. Transfer into a pastry bag, then squeeze some of the mixture into each strawberry. Put graham cracker or animal crackers in a sandwich bag and crush gently into crumbs. Sprinkle the crumbs on top of the strawberries and impress your friends with how fancy you are!

NOTE:

Go DIY by cutting off the bottom corner of a sandwich bag for a makeshift pastry bag! Not gonna lie: that's always how we make these!

CHOCOLATE DIP STICKS

Salty and sweet—a great combination to
keep your engine running smoothly.

MAKES 4 SERVINGS

- 1 (12-ounce) bag vegan chocolate chips
- 1 (10-ounce) bag pretzel rods
- Chocolate or rainbow sprinkles (optional)

Line a tray with wax paper and set aside. Put the chocolate chips in a bowl and nuke for 1 minute. Stir. Heat for another 30 seconds, if necessary, and stir till smooth. Hold each pretzel rod over the bowl while you spoon the melted chocolate over it. Hold the pretzels over another bowl and top with sprinkles. Place the pretzels on the lined tray and put in the fridge until cool.

CHOCOLATE CHIP HUG IN A MUG

This warm and gooey cookie concoction will make you so happy that you'll start giving out free hugs on campus. Seriously, stop making the sign. It's just a sugar high.

MAKES 1 SERVING

- 1 tablespoon vegan margarine
- 1 tablespoon brown sugar
- 1 tablespoon sugar
- ¼ teaspoon vanilla extract
- ⅛ teaspoon salt
- 1 teaspoon Ener-G Egg Replacer mixed with 1 ½ tablespoons water
- 3 tablespoons flour
- 2 tablespoons vegan semisweet chocolate chips

Put the margarine in a microwave-safe mug and nuke until melted, about 20 to 25 seconds. Add the brown sugar, sugar, vanilla, and salt, and mix until combined. Pour the egg replacer into the cookie mug, mix well, then stir in the flour. Add the chocolate chips and give the mixture a few more stirs. Microwave on high for 50 to 60 seconds. Eat right away to enjoy the soft meltiness (though it will be hot), or let it sit for 10 minutes. Eat with a spoon!

BACHELORETTE PARTY BERRIES

Have an engaged friend? Congratulate her on getting her MRS degree by making these bangin' berries. Then make her see how many she can fit in her mouth at once.

MAKES 8 SERVINGS

- 1 (12-ounce) bag vegan chocolate chips
- 1 pound strawberries
- 8 wooden skewers

Put the chocolate chips in a bowl and nuke for 1 minute. Stir. Heat for another 30 seconds, if necessary, and stir until smooth. Dip the strawberries in the chocolate and place on aluminum foil to dry. Impale a few on each skewer and serve.

BANANA INSTA-GRAHAM S'MORES

Post a pic of this ooey, gooey beauty and
leave your followers wanting s'more(s).

MAKES 4 SERVINGS

- 1 vegan chocolate bar, or ⅓ cup vegan semisweet chocolate chips
- 4 vegan graham cracker sheets
- 2 bananas, sliced

Place some chocolate on top of two pieces of graham cracker and nuke the two ingredients for 30 to 45 seconds. Once the chocolate is melted, take it out and "sandwich" the sliced banana in between. Repeat with the rest of the ingredients.

"TAKE A BREAK" AMBROSIA

Okay, enough Internet for you today. Take a
break and feed your soul—not the trolls.

MAKES 4 SERVINGS

- 2 cups jarred mango, drained
- 1 teaspoon lime juice
- Shredded coconut and chopped pecans, to taste

Put the mango and lime juice in a blender and blend till smooth.
Top with shredded coconut and/or pecan pieces and serve.

DUE DATES

Students live and die by deadlines. Now you can
chew through yours like Godzilla in Tokyo.

MAKES 4 SERVINGS

- ½ cup raw nuts (try peanuts or cashews, but any will work)
- 2 tablespoons cinnamon
- 2 (8-ounce) bags pitted dates

Grind the nuts in a food processor or blender until chopped into small pieces. Add the cinnamon and pulse to combine. Set 13 to 15 dates aside, then add the rest to the blender. Grind again until the dates are about the same size as the nuts. Pour into a bowl and set aside. Cut the reserved dates down the long side in order to make room for the filling. Pinch small bits of the mixture together and stuff the dates. Eat.

FAKE BLONDS

We don't care if you highlight as long as you fake your baking skills here (no one will know this is from the microwave!).

MAKES 4 SQUARES

- ⅔ cup sugar
- ½ cup applesauce
- ¼ cup canola oil
- 1 teaspoon vanilla extract
- 1 cup whole wheat flour
- ¼ cup cocoa powder
- ½ teaspoon salt
- ½ cup vegan chocolate chips

Put the sugar, applesauce, canola oil, and vanilla in a large bowl and mix well. In another bowl, mix the flour, cocoa powder, and salt. Add the dry ingredients to the wet ingredients, stirring just until the dry ingredients are wet. Add the chocolate chips and stir a few times to incorporate. Pour into a baking dish that's been sprayed with cooking spray. Nuke for 4 to 5 minutes. Let cool to harden before cutting into bars.

GEORGIA PEACH COBBLER

You don't have to be a sweet Southern belle to enjoy this dessert, y'all.

—————— MAKES 4 SERVINGS ——————

- 1 (15-ounce) can peaches with syrup
- ¼ cup cornflakes or granola (if using granola, make sure it's broken into small bits)
- ¼ cup quick oats
- 1 tablespoon brown sugar
- ½ teaspoon cinnamon

Remove 1 tablespoon of the syrup from the peaches and set aside. Mix together the cornflakes or granola and oats in a bowl. Put about ¼ of the cereal mixture into a separate bowl, then add ⅓ of the peaches (including the syrup). Repeat the layers, ending with the cereal mixture on top. Sprinkle with the brown sugar and cinnamon and drizzle the reserved tablespoon of syrup on top. Nuke for about 2 minutes, until hot. Let cool for a few minutes before digging in.

MELON HEAD GRANITA

A cross between a snow cone and a sorbet, this
chill treat is so worth the brain freeze.

— MAKES 4 SERVINGS —

- 4 cups seedless watermelon chunks
- ½ cup sugar
- 1 tablespoon lemon juice

Puree all the ingredients in a blender until smooth. Pour into a
shallow, wide pan and freeze for 1 hour. Scrape the sides with a fork,
down to the bottom several times, then freeze for an additional
hour. Repeat the scraping and freeze for 1 more hour. Remove
from the freezer, scrape with a fork, and serve immediately.

BANANA HAMMOCK BALLS

Full of tropical fruits and nuts, the only thing missing is a hammock. What were you thinking?

―――――――― MAKES 4 PIECES ――――――――

- 2 ripe bananas
- 1 cup shredded sweetened coconut
- ½ cup chopped dates
- 1 ½ tablespoons cocoa powder

Mash the bananas in a bowl. Add the other ingredients and then form the mixture into balls. Nuke in the microwave for 1 minute or until heated through.

HAPPY BANANA-VERSARY ICE CREAM

The traditional gift for a first-month anniversary is bananas. Okay, we're making that up, but it's still a really sweet treat to share with your new SO.

MAKES 2 SERVINGS

- 4 frozen bananas (peeled and cut into chunks before freezing)
- 1 to 2 tablespoons almond milk (or other nondairy milk)
- 1 to 2 tablespoons creamy peanut butter (optional)

Put frozen banana chunks and milk into a blender and blend well. It'll look chunky at first, but keep on blending and it'll become a nice, smooth, creamy consistency. Add peanut butter and blend more, until well combined. You can eat the ice cream right away at a soft-serve consistency or put it in the freezer for at least an hour to develop a more traditional ice cream texture.

ICE CREAM FRIZZLE DRIZZLE

Best to use at our favorite type of bar—a
vegan ice cream sundae bar!

— MAKES 4 SERVINGS —

- 1 cup frozen berries
- 1 tablespoon powdered sugar
- ½ teaspoon dried mint
- ⅛ teaspoon vanilla

Blend all the ingredients together in a blender. Pour on top of ice cream, sorbet, cake, or another sweet of your choice and serve.

NOON IN CANCUN FROZEN YOGURT

Reminisce about that spring break trip to Mexico with a bowl of fruity, cool, and creamy goodness.

— MAKES 4 SERVINGS —

- ½ cup vegan yogurt (your favorite fruit flavor)
- ¼ cup canned orange slices, drained
- ¼ cup canned pineapple chunks, drained
- ¼ cup orange juice
- Sprinkle of coconut

Put the yogurt, oranges, pineapple, and orange juice in a blender and blend until smooth. Pour into a bowl and stir in the coconut. Freeze for at least 1 hour before eating.

CREAMY BANANA-WAFER PUDDING

Any recipe with pudding is an automatic crowd-pleaser.

--- MAKES 4 SERVINGS ---

- ¾ cup vegan vanilla wafers
- 2 bananas, sliced
- 1 ½ cups cold soy or almond milk
- 1 (3.4-ounce) package instant vegan vanilla pudding mix

Put the wafers in the bottom of a 9 × 9-inch dish and top with half of the banana slices. Prepare the pudding by placing the cold milk and dry pudding mix in a blender and blending gently until smooth. Pour the pudding on top of the banana-wafer "crust." Let set in the fridge for a couple of hours. Top with extra banana slices and serve.

FOOD OF THE GODDESSES

Pamper yourself with these tasty morsels.

———— MAKES 4 SERVINGS ————

- 3 ½ cups vegan cake or cookie crumbs (just crumble some soft cookies or cake)
- 1 ½ cups powdered sugar
- 6 tablespoons orange juice
- 5 ½ tablespoons vegan margarine
- ⅓ cup shredded coconut

Stir together the cake crumbs and powdered sugar in a large bowl. Add the orange juice and margarine. Mix well, then form 1-inch balls. Roll the balls in the shredded coconut, place on a large plate, and chill in the refrigerator for an hour, until firm.

MIAMI BEACH PUDDING

It's like spring break for your mouth!

— MAKES 4 SERVINGS —

- 1 (14-ounce) package soft tofu
- ½ cup sugar
- 1 ½ teaspoons vanilla extract
- ½ cup shredded coconut

Whip the tofu, sugar, and vanilla extract in a blender until stiff and creamy. Fold the coconut into the tofu mixture in a bowl. Pour the pudding into parfait glasses or individual dessert bowls and chill. For an extra treat, serve topped with chocolate sauce.

POSEUR PINEAPPLE PIE

Looks like pineapple pie, but don't be fooled by
this suspiciously docile dessert. Underneath it all,
it's just fruit trying to be something it's not.

─── MAKES 6 SERVINGS ───

- 1 (20-ounce) can crushed pineapple, refrigerated and undrained
- ½ tablespoon cornstarch
- 1 (20-ounce) can sliced peaches, drained
- 1 cup fresh blueberries
- ½ pint fresh strawberries, cut up
- 1 vegan piecrust

Put 3 tablespoons of the cold pineapple juice and the cornstarch in a dish and mix together until the cornstarch has dissolved. Add the rest of the pineapple juice, along with the pineapple, and nuke for 5 minutes or until bubbling and thickened. Set aside. Arrange the peaches, blueberries, and strawberries in the crust and cover with the pineapple sauce. Refrigerate for at least 1 hour before serving.

CHEAPSKATE DATES

A small price to pay for a big reward. Don't you
wish all of your dates were this cheap and easy?

———— MAKES 4 SERVINGS ————

- ½ (8-ounce) container vegan cream cheese
- ¼ cup powdered sugar
- 2 tablespoons orange juice
- 1 box whole, pitted dates
- Powdered sugar (optional)

Beat together the cream cheese, powdered sugar, and orange juice in a bowl. Cut each date down the middle and stuff the cream cheese mixture into the date. Refrigerate for at least 30 minutes. Dust with powdered sugar before serving if you wanna get fancy.

CHOCO-NANNER PARFAIT

Parfait is French for perfect. Say that to those study-abroad hotties over at the languages building and see how they swoon.

MAKES 4 SERVINGS

- 1 ½ cups soy milk
- 1 (3.4-ounce) package instant vegan chocolate pudding mix
- 1 cup crushed vegan cookies or graham crackers
- 2 large bananas, sliced
- ⅓ cup vegan chocolate chips

Mix the milk and dry pudding. Refrigerate for 10 minutes. Layer some of the crushed cookies/graham crackers, banana slices, and pudding in a tall glass. Top with some chocolate chips and refrigerate for 1 hour. Repeat in additional glasses until all the ingredients are used.

BLUEBERRY PIE DUMP CAKE

As with Dumpster diving, all of the good stuff is always at the bottom.

——— MAKES 6 SERVINGS ———

- 1 (21-ounce) can blueberry pie filling
- 1 (8 ½-ounce) can crushed sweetened pineapple, undrained
- 1 (9-ounce) package vegan yellow cake mix (try Duncan Hines—many are vegan)
- ½ cup coarsely chopped walnuts or pecans
- ⅓ cup vegan margarine, melted

Spread blueberry pie filling evenly into a cake dish, then spoon pineapple (including the juice) on top of it. Sprinkle cake mix evenly over the fruit, then sprinkle the nuts on top. Drizzle melted margarine as evenly as possible over all. Set the cake dish in the center of the microwave, then nuke uncovered for 10 minutes. The mixture should be boiling throughout. Set the dish on a heat-resistant flat surface and allow to cool before serving.

BREAKUP PUDDING

Nothing mends a broken heart quite like sitting in
bed in your pajamas, watching hours of reality TV,
and eating an entire bowl of this chocolate pudding.

MAKES 4 SERVINGS

- 1 (14-ounce) package firm silken tofu, crumbled
- ½ cup, plus 2 tablespoons sugar
- ½ cup unsweetened cocoa powder
- 2 ½ teaspoons vanilla extract
- Pinch of salt

Blend all ingredients in a food processor or blender until creamy
and thick. Chill.

CHOCO-AVO PUDDING

Yeah, yeah, we know it sounds weird. But in this case, weird is good and damned tasty.

— MAKES 1 SERVING —

- 1 avocado, peeled and pitted
- ¼ cup cocoa powder
- ¼ cup sugar
- 1 teaspoon vanilla extract

Place all ingredients into a blender and blend until creamy. That's it!

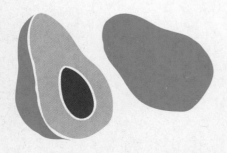

NO-BAKE
CHOCOLATE CAKE

No oven? No problem. Help yourself to some Easy Bake lovin' straight from your microwave oven.

MAKES 4 SERVINGS

- ¼ cup banana, mashed
- ¼ cup soy milk
- ¼ cup sugar
- 3 tablespoons vegan margarine, softened
- 1 teaspoon vanilla extract
- ½ cup flour
- 2 tablespoons cocoa powder
- ¼ teaspoon baking powder
- Dash of salt

Spray a medium bowl with nonstick spray and set aside. Combine the banana, soy milk, sugar, margarine, and vanilla extract in a separate bowl, and stir. Combine the flour, cocoa powder, baking powder, and salt in another bowl. Stir the dry mixture into the wet one until smooth, then pour into the greased bowl. Cover and cook in the microwave on high for 2 to 2 ½ minutes or until cake springs back when touched. Let the cake cool for 5 minutes. When it's cooled, cover the bowl with a plate and turn both bowl and plate upside down so the cake falls onto the plate.

MALLOW-NUT TRUFFLES

All your favorite snack foods in one bite.
It doesn't get any better than that.

————— MAKES 4 SERVINGS —————

- 1 cup plain popped popcorn
- 1 cup salted peanuts
- 1 cup vegan marshmallow topping (we like Smucker's and Suzanne's Ricemellow Creme)
- 1 pound vegan semisweet chocolate, broken into pieces

Coat a baking pan with oil. Gently mix the popcorn, peanuts, and marshmallow topping together and form into little mounds on the pan. Put the chocolate pieces in a bowl and nuke for 1 minute. Stir. Heat for another 30 seconds if necessary and stir until smooth. Pour the melted chocolate over each little mound, covering completely. Refrigerate until chocolate is set.

COUCH SURFER SPONGE PUDDING

Super-smooth banana pudding that's easy to make and easy to swallow—unlike the fact that your couch-crashing buddy won't get off your futon.

MAKES 4 SERVINGS

- ¼ cup sugar
- ¼ cup vegan margarine
- ¼ cup banana, mashed
- 2 tablespoons soy milk
- ½ cup self-rising flour

In a medium bowl, mix together the sugar and margarine until smooth. Add the banana and soy milk and, while stirring, slowly add the flour, mixing until all the ingredients are well blended. Cover and nuke for 3 ½ minutes or until the pudding is slightly congealed. Eat.

LOCO-COCOA SNACK CAKE

Crazy fast and delicious.

MAKES 4 SERVINGS

- 1 ½ cups all-purpose flour
- 1 cup sugar
- ½ cup unsweetened cocoa powder
- 1 teaspoon baking soda
- ½ teaspoon salt
- 1 cup water
- ½ cup vegetable oil
- 2 teaspoons vanilla extract
- 2 tablespoons white vinegar

Combine the flour, sugar, cocoa powder, baking soda, and salt in a bowl. Combine the remaining ingredients in a separate bowl, then stir into the flour mixture. Microwave on high for 6 to 7 minutes, rotating a quarter turn twice. Dish is cooked through when a fork comes out clean when inserted in the center. Let cool for 10 minutes.

CHOCOLATE DORM CAKE

Need to find common ground with someone?
This cake is a great way to start—there's no
problem that chocolate cannot solve.

— MAKES 12 SERVINGS —

- 1 (16.5 ounce) box vegan chocolate cake mix (Duncan Hines has vegan options)
- 1 cup water
- ⅓ cup applesauce
- 1 (8-ounce) container vegan cream cheese, softened
- ¼ cup sugar
- 1 teaspoon vanilla
- 1 (12-ounce) bag vegan chocolate chips

Mix cake mix, water, and applesauce in a bowl until well combined. Pour ¾ of the cake batter into a 9 × 13-inch glass dish, then set aside. In another bowl, stir together the cream cheese, sugar, and vanilla until smooth. Mix in the chocolate chips. Spread the cream cheese mixture evenly over the cake batter. Pour the remaining cake batter on top of cream cheese mixture. Cook uncovered in the microwave for 15 minutes. Rotate the cake while cooking. Watch closely and make sure the cake is cooking evenly. Let cool 5 or 10 minutes, then serve.

MARCHMALLOW MADNESS SQUARES

Graham crackers, chocolate, and
marshmallows. Eat like a baller.

MAKES 10 SQUARES

- 30 vegan graham crackers, divided into squares
- 1 (12-ounce) package vegan semisweet chocolate chips
- 6 tablespoons vegan margarine
- 1 (12.25-ounce) jar vegan marshmallow topping (we like Smucker's and Suzanne's Ricemellow Creme)
- 1 (13-ounce) box puffed rice cereal

Spray a 9 × 13-inch pan with cooking spray. Place 15 graham squares on the bottom of the pan, overlapping slightly. Set aside. Put the chocolate chips and 2 tablespoons of the margarine in a bowl and nuke for 2 minutes, then stir until melted. Spread half of the melted chocolate over the graham squares. Nuke the remaining 4 tablespoons of margarine in a bowl for 45 seconds or until melted. Add the marshmallow topping and stir until smooth. Add the cereal and mix to coat. Press the cereal mixture firmly over the graham squares in the pan. Drizzle with the remaining melted chocolate. Immediately top with the remaining 15 graham squares. Cool and then dive in!

PINK PRINCESS PIE

Charm those snotty girls on the campus
events committee with this sweet and creamy
dessert while you make your case for allowing
a vegan bake sale during welcome week.

MAKES 8 SERVINGS

- 1 (12-ounce) can pink lemonade concentrate
- 2 ½ cups vegan vanilla ice cream
- 1 (9-inch) vegan graham cracker piecrust

Blend the lemonade concentrate for 30 seconds in the blender. Spoon in the ice cream and blend until combined. Pour into the crust and freeze overnight.

SNOWBALLS FROM HELL

The odds of these peachy keen popsicles lasting once your roommates know about them? A snowball's chance in hell. Like your odds of getting backstage to meet your fave band.

―――――――――― MAKES 4 SERVINGS ――――――――――

- 1 ½ cups canned peaches, drained
- ¼ cup peach preserves
- 1 tablespoon coconut flakes
- 1 tablespoon sugar

Put everything in a blender and blend. Scoop 2 tablespoons of the mixture into each cube of an ice cube tray. Freeze until almost firm, then insert a toothpick in each one and freeze the rest of the way.

SCREAMING PUDDING PIE

One bite of this, and your taste buds—and maybe your crush—will be screaming for more.

— MAKES 8 SERVINGS —

- 1 cup cold soy milk
- 1 cup vegan chocolate ice cream, softened
- 1 (3.4-ounce) package instant vegan chocolate pudding mix
- 1 (9-inch) vegan graham cracker piecrust

Mix together the milk and ice cream in a large bowl. Add the pudding and mix for 1 to 2 minutes. Pour into the crust and refrigerate for a couple of hours.

SHAKE-AND-MAKE FRO YO

Don't settle for that diseased dairy crap from the ice cream stand down the street. Make your own!

——— MAKES 4 SERVINGS ———

- 3 to 4 pounds of ice cubes
- 6 tablespoons rock salt
- 1 cup vanilla soy milk
- 2 tablespoons sugar
- ½ tablespoon vanilla extract
- Vegan cones

Fill a gallon-size plastic, resealable bag half full with ice. Add the rock salt and set aside. Pour the soy milk, sugar, and vanilla into a pint-size plastic resealable bag, and seal. Place the pint-size plastic bag inside the gallon-size plastic bag and seal. Shake the bag for 5 to 7 minutes. Remove the pint-size bag from the larger bag. Use scissors to cut away a corner from the pint-size bag, then squeeze the soy ice cream into the cones, soft-serve style.

NOTE:
. . . .

Use oven mitts to prevent your hands from getting too cold.

INDEX

ABOUT THE AUTHORS

PEOPLE FOR THE ETHICAL TREATMENT OF ANIMALS (PETA) is the largest animal rights organization in the world. PETA focuses its attention on the four areas in which the largest numbers of animals suffer the most intensely for the longest periods of time: on factory farms, in laboratories, in the clothing trade, and in the entertainment industry. It also works on a variety of other issues, including the cruel killing of beavers, birds, and other "pests," and the abuse of backyard dogs.

PETA works through public education, cruelty investigations, research, animal rescue, legislation, special events, celebrity involvement, outreach, and protest campaigns.

Marta Holmberg has worked to help high school and college students go vegan for the past ten years and is the senior director of Youth Outreach & Campaigns at PETA. She's been a vegetarian since she was four years old and went vegan in college. She lives in Los Angeles.

Starza Kolman went veg in middle school after being forced to take Hunter's Education. She is known for her saucy attitude and uncanny ability to create culinary masterpieces without actually cooking.

For more information on going vegan, please visit peta2.com.